THE WORD FOR EVERY SEASON

Reflections on the Lectionary Readings

(CYCLE B)

Dianne Bergant, CSA

Paulist Press
New York/Mahwah, NJ

Most of these reflections originally appeared in "The Word" column of *America* magazine.

Cover photographs by Anton deFlon and Nancy deFlon
Cover design by Sharyn Banks
Book design by Lynn Else

Library of Congress Cataloging-in-Publication Data

Bergant, Dianne.
    The Word for every season : reflections on the lectionary readings (cycle B) / Dianne Bergant.
        p. cm.
    ISBN-13: 978-0-8091-4545-4 (alk. paper)
    1. Church year meditations. I. Title.
    BX2170.C55B44 2008
    242'.3—dc22

                                                            2008004382

Published by Paulist Press
997 Macarthur Boulevard
Mahwah, New Jersey 07430

www.paulistpress.com

Printed and bound in the
United States of America

Contents

Introduction

The Catholic Bible Movement of the 1950s introduced us to what is known as the "historical-critical approach" to interpreting the Bible. This approach opened us to exciting new insights into the historical background of the stories with which we had become so familiar. What had often seemed baffling could now be better explained, and this without losing the religious mystery behind the biblical passage. Soon, even grade school children were devouring the fruits of this new method of interpretation.

Within the more recent past, we have gleaned new insights into biblical interpretation from various methods of literary criticism. This approach is not primarily interested in the concerns of the original author or the original biblical communities. It maintains that, once it leaves the original situation, the biblical text has a message in its own right, independent of the specific meaning of the author or the early communities. This is similar to the case with music: One need not consult Bach to interpret one of his fugues. Everything needed for such an interpretation can be found in the score itself. So, everything needed for an interpretation of the Bible can be found within the Bible itself.

Over the years we have found that the employment of such interpretive approaches has enriched our understanding of the scriptures in ways too numerous to list. However, we maintain that the scriptures are more than religious texts meant to be studied with an eye to their importance to an ancient people, or as an example of well-crafted religious literature. We believe that the religious message that they contain is the foundation of our faith, and that somehow that religious message is meant to shape our own religious identity and to influence our behavior. We want to know what that message might mean for us today.

The reflections collected in this book are an attempt to address this final concern: What might that message mean for us today? These reflections spring from a careful examination of the lectionary readings for every Sunday and Solemnity of the liturgical year. Though at times historical or literary information might be offered, the focus here is on prayerful musing on the meaning that message might have for us today. It is in ways such as this that the word takes root in our hearts in and out of season.

Advent

FIRST SUNDAY OF ADVENT

Readings:
Isa 63:16b–17, 19b; 64:2–7;
Ps 80:2–3, 15–16, 18–19;
1 Cor 1:3–9; Mark 13:33–37

THERE'S A NEW WORLD COMING!

We spend so much of life waiting. As children, we could hardly wait for birthdays, free days, and holidays; we could hardly wait to grow up. Now as adults, we wait for buses and trains; we wait in doctors' offices and government agencies; we wait for our turn on the golf course or the tennis court; we wait to get into the theater. Some people even wait to die. At times we wait for something to happen; at other times we wait for something to stop happening. In either case, waiting for the future to unfold is a common human experience.

Advent is a time of waiting. But waiting for what? Surely, it is not simply a time of waiting for the birth of Christ, for that event has already taken place. Nor is it really a time of waiting for the end of the world, as some have claimed. The readings of the season tell us that Advent is a time of waiting for the appearance of the reign of God. We believe that this reign dawned for us with the birth of Christ, and that is why we look forward to the feast of Christmas and celebrate its importance. We believe that this reign issues in a new world of grace, and that is why we reflect on the end of the old world. The reign of God is always unfolding before us, and so we are always looking for its further appearance; we are always hoping for a time of reconciliation and genuine peace, a time of mutual respect and cooperation. Advent is the time of waiting for this new world to appear.

We long for such a new world because we can no longer tolerate the one in which we live. The present world is one of violence and hatred, of dishonesty and greed, a world that seems to prey on the most vulnerable. From the midst of such pain, Isaiah invites us to cry out to God in complaint: Why have you not protected us? Why have you permitted such evils to occur? Why have you allowed things to get so bad?

Though today we seldom use formal lament in our public prayer, the ancient Israelites certainly did. They seem to have had no problem complaining to God. And why not? To whom else, if not to God, should we turn when we are oppressed and overburdened, and feel hopeless? Who better than God can remedy the personal and social ills that we must endure? Religious souls lament the apparent absence of God in the workings of the world. Tender hearts lament the fate of those who have been afflicted or marginalized in society. Broken spirits lament the suffering that touches every life. Through the ages believers have cried out: "Where is God?" or directing their complaint to God have demanded: "How long, O Lord?" The readings for this first Sunday of Advent direct us to acknowledge the difficulties that face us in life, difficulties that we often find so crushing. Advent is a time to lament these difficulties.

Though the readings direct us to acknowledge our pain, they do not allow us to become fixated on it. Instead, we are invited to turn our gaze to the hope of a brighter future. The images of God employed in these readings encourage us to do so. The very character of these images enables us to move from our initial complaint to expressions of confidence. Isaiah addresses God both as father who has given us life and who cares for us, and as artisan who has fashioned us as works of art. The psalmist depicts God as a shepherd who is attentive to the sheep, as a vinedresser who works diligently for the health and productivity of the vines, as an imperial ruler and a military captain, both of whom are committed to the welfare of their people. These images are meant to assure us of God's solicitous concern. Our waiting for a new world may be tedious and sometimes even discouraging, but we should not be disheartened for God is there for us.

When will the revelation of Jesus Christ appear? When will this new world arrive? When will the Day of the Lord dawn? We do not know for sure, and so we must wait with patient expectation; we must wait in joyful hope that it will come soon. And what should we do while we wait? In the gospel story the servants do not wait idly. They assume responsibility for the work of the household. Today we are responsible for the natural world of which we are a part, for the society to which we belong, and for the work of the church of which we are members. As overwhelming as this task may seem, Paul reminds us that we have all of the gifts and talents that we need to live faithfully in this world: "You are not lacking in any spiritual gift as you wait for the revelation of our Lord Jesus Christ."

Pregnant with expectation, we are admonished to prepare for the day of fulfillment. We wait for that day in partnership with others who wait. This means that in our waiting we are vigilant for justice, compassionate toward those who lament, and, yes, forgiving of those who wrong us. We live between the time of Christ's first coming and the time of final fulfillment, an "in-between" time of ambiguity and hope. We believe that we have a future worth waiting for, worth working toward. Relying on God's promises to us, we firmly believe that there is indeed a new world coming, and the one in which we now live is coming to an end. We might not know exactly when it is coming, but it might be right around the bend!

Praying with Scripture

- What can you do to assure that weapons of war will be converted to implements of peace?

- Where in your life can you replace rivalry and jealousy with sentiments of kindness and understanding?

- How ready are you to meet God, not merely in death, but in life?

SECOND SUNDAY OF ADVENT
Readings:
Isa 40:1–5, 9–11; Ps 85:9–14;
2 Pet 3:8–14; Mark 1:1–8

DO YOU HEAR VOICES?

The wilderness, which can seduce us with its beauty and its majesty, has many faces. In one part of the country its dense forests and lush vegetation can fill up our senses with its luxuriance. In another part, its stark barrenness can purge us of any shallow affectation, while its grandeur can still take away our breath. The wilderness is a place of wonder and exploration, a place of respite from the struggles of the world, and a place of rejuvenation of both body and soul. This is true, of course, unless we are lost in it. Then the wilderness is a place of dread and terror, for it will support our lives only if we possess the requisite survival skills. Without such skills, we can find ourselves at the mercy of an apparently disinterested, even hostile, environment.

Today the calm of our lives is startled by voices from the wilderness. In the reading from the prophet Isaiah we hear one crying out for the construction of a passable route through the desert; from another desert we hear John the Baptist's unsettling call for repentance. Recently we have been involved in armed conflict in a land marked by expanses of unfamiliar wilderness, and we face the possibility of further confrontation in yet another desert-land. The challenges posed by the wilderness, whether that wilderness is a geographical expanse or some form of metaphorical reference, can cut to the core of our lives. It is important to be prepared for an encounter not only within the wilderness but also with the wilderness itself. We now know that we cannot disregard the challenges that it presents, regardless of how we might presume to be ready to face any obstacle.

What do these reflections have to do with Advent? Everything! Our calendars may suggest that Advent is the season of preparation for the celebration of the Nativity. However, the

Advent readings themselves broaden our view and insist that we are really anticipating the coming of the reign of God into our lives. They further declare that we will have to experience the discomfort of the unfamiliar before we enter this new reign. The image of the wilderness suggests that we will be called upon to strip ourselves of whatever will prevent us from moving forward.

Isaiah uses the metaphor of road construction to speak of this stripping. He is not describing minor repairs, such as filling in potholes or refurbishing curbs. He is calling for major reconfiguration of the terrain. He declares that the valleys must be filled in and the mountains must be brought low, the rugged land should be made a plain and the rough country should be changed into a broad valley. Isaiah is calling for serious transformation of the landscape of our lives.

Though he quotes the passage from Isaiah, John the Baptist is more theological as he calls for "a baptism of repentance for the forgiveness of sins." This baptism is not sacramental, as we Christians know it, but an ancient Jewish devotional practice, which included an acknowledgment of sinfulness and a commitment to a change of life. John's message of transformation is quite direct: Repent! He challenges us. Acknowledge your sinfulness, your anger and hatred and desire for revenge, your obsession with power and your manipulation and abuse of others, your greed and unwillingness to help those in need.

The author of 2 Peter echoes this call for repentance. Picking up the theme of last Sunday, he then proclaims that there is indeed a new world on the horizon, a new heaven and a new earth. He too speaks of the new life that will be lived in the reign of God. It will be a life of holiness and devotion. He also says something that seems a bit confusing. We are told to wait and at the same time to hasten the coming of this new day. This is not a contradiction; it is a paradox. We are to wait for it, because it comes to us from God; but we are also to live in such a way that our very manner of living is evidence of its presence among us. Once again we are faced with the need to reform our lives.

As difficult as this change of heart might appear to be, it is our way of entering into the anticipated reign of God. The focus of today's readings is not so much on the sacrifices we may have to make as it is on the transformation that God has in store for us.

The dawning of the reign of God will be a new day in the future. It will be a time when kindness and truth meet, when justice and peace kiss, when truth springs out of the earth, and justice looks down from heaven. Advent is a time of serious preparation for this new way of living in the world. The voices in today's readings all call us to move toward this new world.

Praying with Scripture

- Reflect on the ways God is calling you to reform.

- Ask God for the help you need to alter the landscape of your life.

- Place your fears before God and trust that, with God's help, you can indeed shape a new heaven and a new earth.

THIRD SUNDAY OF ADVENT
Readings:
Isa 61:1–2a, 10–11; Luke 1:46–50, 53–54;
1 Thess 5:16–24; John 1:6-8, 19–28

THE PEOPLE WHO WALK UPSIDE DOWN

When Alice fell through the rabbit hole into Wonderland, she was convinced that she had fallen right through the earth and was destined to come out where people would be upside down. She referred to such reversals as *antipathies,* though she did wonder whether or not that was the right word. She may not have chosen the correct word, but she was on target when it came to identifying the way we feel when our world is turned upside down. That is, of course, when the reversal that we experience resembles the collapse of the stock market. We would be overcome by entirely different emotions if we had won the lottery. When she finally landed, Alice discovered that the world was not upside down, but it certainly was out of proportion to her size. She had to change, to get smaller in order to enter that mysterious world.

The Third Sunday of Advent invites us into a world of reversals, a world where the captives are freed, where the hungry are filled, and where the rich are sent away empty. It is certainly a world where things are turned upside down. From the point of view of social order, such reversals could be considered *antipathies*. From God's point of view, however, they are the signs of transformation. In order to appreciate the strength of today's message from Isaiah, we must remember that he was speaking to people who were dispossessed, people in need of a message of hope, a promise of some kind of economic reversal. This same description of reversal is found in the passage from Luke. There we see that the lowly enjoy the blessings that God promised long ago.

It is not that God wants to make us unhappy by turning our world upside down. Rather, God offers us the possibility of a new world. The Wonderland to which we are invited is not some mad tea party attended by an array of strange guests. It is a world established in justice and peace, a world in which all will hear the glad tidings of salvation. It is a world in which everyone can enjoy the happiness of the bride and bridegroom or relish the fruits of the luxurious garden. The dramatic metaphors that Isaiah employs are not meant simply to be poetic flights of fancy. They capture the essence of what we are experiencing internally far better than straightforward prose can. A wedding is certainly a sign of a new and transformative life, just as a sumptuous garden typifies bountiful sustenance.

In order to enter the mysterious new world that lies before us, we, like Alice, might have to undergo some kind of change. Paul is conscious of our need of transformation, for he prays that the God of peace will make us perfectly holy, blameless at the coming of the Lord. In line with this thinking, the basis of the preaching of John the Baptist is repentance. His message today is the same as it was last week: Make straight the way of the Lord! Get rid of any obstacle that might deter his arrival. Eliminate from your lives the greed that impoverishes others, the arrogance that tries to set you above the rest, the power that makes you abusive, the selfishness that turns you in on your own concerns alone.

Today we are all aware of the destructive evil that such attitudes have spawned. We suffer the consequences of their corrosive power. Our faith reminds us, however, that we do not have to remain victims of these forces. There is a far better way of living in the world, and on this Third Sunday of Advent we stand at its threshold. However, we are faced with a challenge. Are we willing to step forward? Or are we afraid to have our world turned upside down? Are we the poor who will hear the good news of reversal, or are we the ones responsible for their poverty? Are we the bro-kenhearted who will be healed, or have we broken their hearts? Are we the captives who will be freed, or are we the captors who have restrained them? On what side of the reversals do we find ourselves?

Advent is a time to search our hearts, to discover where we need to change, both individually and as a community. It is a time of expectation, for we are told that there is one who has the power to heal our personal brokenness, to heal our fractured families, to heal our troubled church, to heal our bleeding world. Paul tells us that he is coming; John tells us that he is already in our midst. His presence among us should make us rejoice; the saving power that he brings should give us confidence. If we open our hearts to this saving power, we can indeed transform our society; we can renew our church; we can work toward peace in the world. We can really turn our world upside down.

Praying with Scripture

- Pray for the light to recognize what in your life should be turned "upside down" and for the courage to do it.

- Rejoice in the realization that Christ is in our midst, ready to work through us to heal our world.

- Make the passage from Luke your own prayer, realizing how it does indeed reflect God's goodness to you.

FOURTH SUNDAY OF ADVENT
Readings:
2 Sam 7:1–5, 8b–12, 14a, 16; Ps 89:2–5, 27, 29;
Rom 16:25–27; Luke 1:26–38

WELCOME TO THE REAL WORLD

Today we move out of the realm of religious testimony into the real world of history. Both the first and the third readings situate Jesus within the family of David. They do this not simply to look back into history, as interesting as that may be. They do it in order to underscore the historical grounding of the mystery of the incarnation. We know that Jesus was one of us because we can pinpoint his historical lineage.

The house of David to which Jesus belonged had skeletons in its closet. It traced its origin to Judah, one of the twelve sons of Jacob. Judah himself reneged on his responsibility to ensure an heir for his deceased son, and so his daughter-in-law Tamar tricked him into impregnating her (Gen 38). Later in history, the Moabite Ruth married Boaz because a closer relative spurned a similar responsibility to Ruth's late husband (Ruth 4). The sons born of these two women became the ancestors of David, who was himself guilty of adultery and murder (2 Sam 11). Such was the "illustrious" family into which Jesus was born.

Despite the sinfulness of this family, it was the one chosen by God to be the instrument of blessing for others. The first reading describes how this was to take place: "I will raise up your heir after you, sprung from your loins, and I will make his kingdom firm." Down through the centuries, Davidic kings ruled God's people. Then, this promise was fulfilled in a way that no one could have imagined. Mary is told that the child she will bear "will be called the Son of the Most High, and the Lord God will give him the throne of David his father."

We may be so familiar with aspects of the incarnation that we fail to recognize the incongruities surrounding it. The very idea that the divine would actually assume human flesh is beyond comprehension. Yet our Christian faith claims that Jesus is indeed the Son of God and was also one of us according to the flesh. Human nature, not just his human nature but ours as well, has been deemed worthy to hold the glory of God. We sometimes concentrate on the virginal body of Mary as the sacred vessel within which this mystery unfolded. In choosing her human body, however, God was really choosing our human nature.

Furthermore, God did not choose people renowned for their constancy in virtue or steadfastness in fidelity. Perhaps this is because there is no such perfect family. Whatever the case may be, Jesus was born of a family in which some people frequently misused their positions of power and authority; others gained their rights by means of deception; still others seemed oblivious to the working of God in their lives. God chose a family not unlike our own families. In other words, the incarnation occurred within the real world of flesh and blood, of weak and sinful women and men.

God chooses people who seldom fit the criteria that we might employ. David was the youngest son of the family, the one who looked after the sheep. Not even his father thought to present him to the prophet as a possible contender for the throne (1 Sam 16:11). Even Mary, a simple woman from a backwater town in Galilee, was an unlikely choice. She was an unknown individual from a town that was considered insignificant ("Can anything good come from Nazareth?" [John 1:46]). The mystery of which Paul speaks today is not only the *fact* of the incarnation ("the mystery kept secret for long ages"), but also the *means* whereby it came to be ("according to the command of the eternal God"). The incarnation of God, as mysterious as it may be, is grounded in the very human nature that we all share. It is clear that God chooses the weak of the world to confound the strong.

The waiting of Advent is over. In the face of the impossible, God works the possible. Mary is asked to believe this. She is open and accepting. She is asked to believe something else equally impossible. The old and barren Elizabeth is pregnant, for nothing is impossible with God. What we have been waiting for all Advent is now revealed. We have been waiting for the realization of the promise made to David. We have been waiting for Mary's "yes." Her "yes" took place in history, but radically transformed history. There is a now unimaginable future for all people, a future that comes from God. Salvation is created among us, and the fate of history is altered by a godly presence. With David we awaited it, with the nations we longed for it, with Mary we now behold it. This messy world of ours, the real world of human history, is now charged with the grandeur of God. And so we can greet our Lord Jesus Christ with the words: Welcome to the real world!

Praying with Scripture

- Reflect on the dignity that is yours as a human being.

- What might you have to do to live up to that dignity?

- Think about how God might be calling you to act as an agent of saving grace in the lives of others.

Christmas Season

CHRISTMAS (B)

Readings:
(Midnight) Isa 9:1–6; Ps 96:1–3, 11–13;
Titus 2:11–14; Luke 2:1–14; (Dawn) Isa 62:11–12;
Ps 97:1–6, 11–12; Titus 3:4–7; Luke 2:15–20;
(Day) Isa 52:7–10; Ps 98:1–6; Heb 1:1–6;
John 1:1–18

"FOR UNTO US A CHILD IS BORN"

The chorus from Handel's *Messiah* begins with the heart-warming announcement, "For unto us a child is born," and builds to a thunderous declaration, "And his name shall be called Wonderful!" The gospels for the three Masses of Christmas follow the same progression of thought. Images from the first two gospels are captured in many Christmas cards. They depict the quiet countryside of Bethlehem, the proclamation of the angels to the shepherds in the fields, or the stable with Mary and Joseph, and the child in the manger. These scenes are captured in the phrase, "For unto us a child is born." The third gospel lifts us out of history into the realm of mystery. There Jesus is identified as the Word of God, who was present with God in the beginning, through whom all things came to be, and who became flesh. A fitting response to this portrayal would be, "And his name shall be called Wonderful!"

The birth of a baby is always a time of celebration and hope. We have reason to celebrate, for the cynicism that clouds so much of our lives has been dispelled; we have reason to hope that life will be better for the baby, and because of the baby, better for the rest of us. A newborn child has no past, and so every infant is a promise of the future, not simply the future of that particular infant, but the future of us all. When a child is brought into the world, the entire family is changed, and so is the future of that family. Now, anything is possible

The future of us all is on the shoulders of the child at whose birth we rejoice today. With his birth, the new world of promise has been born and God has been proven trustworthy. The question is whether or not we are trustworthy. Will we be faithful to the present and fashion a new world for the future? Will we follow the admonitions that Paul delivered to Titus "to live temperately, justly, and devoutly"? Will we assiduously work for peace and not simply send it as a message on a Christmas card? Will we open our hearts to others all the year long and not merely during this season of generous giving? Will the birth of this child really make a difference in our lives?

This child's birth is shrouded in paradox. Though he was in the beginning with God, he enters into time to be with us; though all things were made through him, he concealed his power under swaddling bands. He came as prince of peace into a world of enmity; he came as light into a world of darkness. Paradoxes such as these remind us that God desires to accomplish in us and in our world marvels that we cannot begin to fathom. Still, we must ask: "What has really changed with his birth? Is there peace? Is there light? Have we been open to receive the marvels that God has in store for us?" The gospel reading of the second Mass recounts how the shepherds went in haste to look for the child, and, having found him, they go out and announce it to everyone they meet. They are examples for us of how to respond to the message of this day. We must go in haste to find the child, and then, by our lives, announce it to everyone we meet.

The new world that this child brings, the restoration that his birth promises, is already unfolding in our midst. Many people go out of their way to care for the needy of the world, not only at Christmastime, but also throughout the entire year. They collect and distribute food and clothing and medical supplies; they protest injustice that is perpetrated against the vulnerable; they volunteer their time and energy, helping to rebuild lives that have been devastated by natural disaster, social upheaval, or war.

If we do not see this new world, perhaps it is because we ourselves are doing nothing to bring it about. Perhaps the peace we wish each other at Christmas is merely a holiday greeting and not a promise to live in peace. Perhaps we have romanticized the poor and the despised shepherds while we ignore the poor and the despised among us. Perhaps our celebration of Christmas is simply the reenactment of a seasonal mystery play rather than the real enactment of God's love for us all. Perhaps our good intentions are packed away with the Christmas decorations, only to be brought out again next year.

If we forget that Christmas is a time of promise, as is the birth of every child, then we will have missed the very core of its message. The child born is the Savior, the Word of God, the Wonder-Counselor, God-Hero, Prince of Peace. The promise was made by God, not by us, and so it is trustworthy. All we have to do is open our hearts to accept it, as we would accept the child that is born to us.

Praying with Scripture

- Reflect on the mystery of God's incomprehensible love in your life.

- How open are you to receive the true mystery of Christmas?

- What new life might you bring into the world?

HOLY FAMILY
Readings:
Sir 3:2–7, 12–14; Ps 128:1–5;
Col 3:12–21; Luke 2:22–40

A RETURN TO FAMILY VALUES

Today we seem deluged with reports of anger, abuse, and even murder at the hands of a family member. Spouses are not attentive to each other; parents neglect children; and children disregard adults. It is time to return to good old-fashioned family values. But what constitutes good old-fashioned family values? Is it the submission of wives, the domineering rule of parents, the intimidation of children? Is there anything universally applicable regarding family values? Or do they differ from generation to generation, culture to culture? Just what are authentic family values?

In response to the threats facing the family unit, various groups claim to be the guardians of traditional family values. However, many of them fail to acknowledge the fundamental changes existing in the family unit itself. Past generations did not have to cope with situations in which both parents were required to work outside of the home; there were very few single parent families; professional day-care was limited to the economically well-to-do; and latchkey children were unheard of. Add to this all of the extracurricular activities in which children and parents alike are involved, and the complexity of contemporary family life becomes quite clear. How can traditional family values be exercised in such circumstances? Today's readings would respond to that question. However, such values might have to be interpreted in new ways.

We must remember that the family is not only the first and perhaps most formative school, but it also is the fundamental ecclesial or church community. It is there that we learn right from wrong; it is there that we first learn to pray together. Paul's admonition to the Christians of Colossae, originally intended for a church community, certainly fits the family unit as well: "Put on...heartfelt compassion, kindness, humility, gentleness, and patience, bearing with one another and forgiving one another.... And over all of these put on love." We are all called to act with this kind of love and respect toward others, whether they are members of the family, the broader society, or the church. All belong to the household of God and are to be treated according to that dignity.

The passage from Sirach has long been considered one of the most moving descriptions of authentic family values. Parents are told to be diligent in raising their children, and adult children are charged to be gentle with their own aging parents. Love, honor, and respect are clearly the bedrock of these family values. Sirach adds another dimension to this family picture. He reminds us that our future is rooted in the rich soil of our past. True wisdom for living is found in the experience of our elders, in those who have already lived wisely. Unfortunately, too often in our culture the elderly are pushed to the margins of social interaction. They are considered the dead past, not the vibrant future. Youth and unrestrained spontaneity are placed before us as models to be emulated. We are impoverished when this occurs.

The gospel describes how the parents of Jesus, themselves faithful to the practices of their Jewish religion, presented to God the child who first had been given to them by God. Like all parents, they must have wondered what his future might hold. Then under their watchful eyes, he "grew and became strong, filled with wisdom; and the favor of God was upon him." The mutual respect undergirding the relationships that existed within the holy family is evident in this short passage. The parents cared for the child and initiated him into the religious practices of their faith. He responded to their care in ways that demonstrated his wisdom and the favor of God that rested upon him. What a perfect example of family values!

Our children are our greatest treasure. They are both the guardians of the past and the promise of the future. To them we entrust our social and cultural traditions, our family customs and secrets, the insights and practices of our faith. Through them the dreams that we dream take forms that we never envisioned. Furthermore, they enrich our lives with hopes and dreams of their own. Their innocence, openness, and vulnerability remind us of what it really means to be human, to view life with fresh excitement rather than jaded cynicism, to be accepting of themselves and of others without bias or prejudice, to acknowledge that we are not self-sufficient but in need of the love and support of others. Do we cherish this treasure? Do we nurture it?

The elderly members of our community are another treasure. The years that they have lived have taught them that miracles do indeed occur. They know the ups and downs of life, and they have survived both. Their weathered faith enables them to recognize the face of God even in the unexpected. Living in the presence of God, they can open themselves and us to receive God's gifts, for they have learned to allow God's promises to overtake them. Both the very young and the elderly can teach us genuine family values.

Praying with Scripture

- Reflect how your own family instilled in you authentic values, and thank God for this.

- What new family values might the contemporary world require of us?

- In what ways might you recommit yourself to your own family, to the family of the church, to the family of all humankind?

SOLEMNITY OF THE BLESSED VIRGIN MARY
Readings:
Num 6:22–27; Ps 67:2–3, 5–6, 8; Gal 4:4–7; Luke 2:16–21

Have I Got a Story to Tell You!

Is it over yet? Are the carols gone from the airwaves? Have the stores dismantled their decorations? Has Christmas been put away to make room for Valentine's Day? It always happens so quickly. We waited and waited for Christmas, and then it came and went in a flash. Maybe it is because Christmas advertising begins before Halloween, and so when Christmas finally comes, we are tired of it. Unfortunately, we no longer allow the mystery of the feast to seep deeply into our lives during "the twelve days of Christmas." We simply sing the song, and we sing it even before Christmas actually arrives. But it did not happen like that for Mary; and we cannot afford to let it happen like that for us. She kept all these things, reflecting on them in her heart—and so must we.

All who heard the shepherds were amazed at the story they had to tell. Who wouldn't be? After all, exceptionally brilliant stars in the heavens and angels proclaiming the birth of a savior are not everyday occurrences. Extraordinary phenomena always capture the attention and imagination of even the most skeptical among us. However, a child in a makeshift crib may not be so unusual. The paradox lies in the fact that the extraordinary phenomena pointed to what appeared to be very commonplace. One can imagine the shepherds running to proclaim: "Have I got a story to tell you!"

The gospel tells us that it was Mary who kept turning the events over and over in her mind, trying to plumb the depths of their meaning. After all, who was she to have been the one chosen to participate in such a marvel? She was a common girl from an undistinguished Galilean village, betrothed to an artisan. There was nothing unusual about any of this. But then her quiet world was disturbed by a heavenly announcement, and from the moment of the angel's unbelievable declaration, she may well have surmised that for the rest of her days she would be living with mystery. And so she kept all these things in her heart.

The straightforward mention of the circumcision of the child points again to the religious observance of Mary and Joseph. This ritual ceremony formally incorporated him into the family of Israel. Mary must have pondered the relevance of this event as well. The angel had told her that her child would "rule over the house of Jacob forever, and of his kingdom there would be no end" (Luke 1:33). It was appropriate that he be circumcised and thus become a legitimate member of the house of Israel in order to accomplish this. But the angel had also told her that he would be "the Son of the Most High" (Luke 1:32). How could an ordinary Israelite boy be the Son of the Most High? Mary would have to ponder this.

The name given to the child was not one decided upon by his parents. Like other individuals who were prominent in the story of God's people (Abraham, Gen 17:5; Jacob/Israel, Gen 35:10; John, Luke 1:13), the child's name was chosen by God (Luke 1:31). The name "Jesus" itself is significant. It is a form of the Hebrew for "Yahweh saves" (see Matt 1:21), and it points to the role that the child will later assume. Mary would probably not be able to grasp the full impact of this name, and so she would reflect on it in her heart.

Paul tells us that as Son of God, Jesus was divine; as son of Mary, he was a human being like the rest of us. Being human as we are, he was able to make us also daughters and sons of God. According to Paul, Jesus' human nature was established through Mary. The Spirit of Jesus is given to us so that we can call God by the intimate term "Abba." This is no less amazing than the report of the shepherds. Mary may not yet have had the insight needed to reflect on this aspect of God's generosity, but we do.

The first day of the New Year is traditionally a day to pray for peace. Unfortunately, in our world today, peace is much more than a seasonal theme. It might conjure up the faces of frightened children dressed in foreign garb and huddled in the ruins of their family home, or the face of a beloved daughter or son in military uniform. Making the prayer of Aaron, found in the first reading for today, our own, we beg God to look upon us kindly and give us peace. Here, again, Mary may well serve as our model. She considered deeply the events of her life, and she sought to follow the promptings of God that were present there. So must we! If peace is to take root in our day and take flesh in our lives, we must reflect on these events in our hearts, and we must follow the promptings of God that are present there. Then the miracle of Christmas will be more than a wondrous story to tell.

Praying with Scripture

- In what way might Mary be a model for contemporary people?

- Spend some time today reflecting on the ways in which God has blessed you.

- As you pray for peace today, commit yourself to a concrete act of peace.

SECOND SUNDAY AFTER CHRISTMAS

Readings:
Sir 24:1–2, 8–12; Ps 147:12–15, 19–20;
Eph 1:3–6, 15–18; John 1:1–5, 9–14

"And Pitched His Tent Among Us"

This Sunday could be called Wisdom Sunday, because all of the readings focus our attention on some aspect of this elusive reality. Wisdom, like so many other characteristics, is difficult to define. However, we know it when we see it. Perhaps the best way to describe it is as insight into life experience. We all have life experience—even newborn infants do—but we do not always have insight into it. That might explain why we often make the same mistake over and over again. In such cases, we simply have not learned from our experience.

We have probably all heard the expression, "Experience is the best teacher." As significant as this expression might be, it is not quite accurate. Actually, experience is the *only* teacher. We learn either from our own experience or from the experience of others. And we all want to learn, to find out how life works, to search for meaning in it. If we could not learn from others we would all have our turn at inventing the wheel, or devising ways of responding to transcendent reality. All cultural folklore, social mores, and religious instruction somehow emerge out of reflection on experience. Someone had to learn how to do things successfully, and these insights were then handed down to the next generation and then to the next and so on. The Books of Proverbs, Wisdom, and Sirach are filled with adages that developed in this way.

There is, however, a dimension to our search for meaning in life that does not seem to be satisfied by the experience of life itself. One of the Israelite sages declared that God "has made everything appropriate to its time, and has put the timeless into [human] hearts, without [anyone] ever discovering, from beginning to end, the work which God had done" (Eccl 3:11). Reflecting on the same sense of incompleteness, St. Augustine cried out: "Our hearts are restless, until they find their rest in you." That indefinable "something" that alone can assuage the longing that lies deep within the human is described in the first reading for this Sunday. It is the Wisdom.

The Wisdom wherein is found the meaning for which we all search is personified in the Bible as a mysterious woman. Though not herself divine, she has immediate access to God. In fact, she was with God in the beginning, created before all ages. That is why she understands all the secrets of creation. Though so closely associated with God, Woman Wisdom is still very close to the people. Her own people admire, exalt, and praise her. And who are these people? The passage tells us that of all the places in the world where she might have established herself, she was directed by God to pitch her tent in Israel. This means that true wisdom is found in the Israelite religious traditions. What a touching image. She lives in a tent much like some of the Israelites did. Such a bold claim was initially made as a challenge to the Hellenizing influence facing the Jewish people. Later a New Testament author incorporated this tradition into his description of Jesus as the eternal Word of God.

"In the beginning was the Word." The Gospel of John opens with these words. It goes on to describe Jesus in ways that include some of the aspects ascribed to Woman Wisdom by the ancient Israelite writers. Like Woman Wisdom, the Word was there in the beginning when God created all things. Furthermore, Jesus is said to make "his dwelling among us." Earlier versions translated the Greek as: "pitched his tent among us." This corresponds more closely to the reference from Sirach. The New Testament writer clearly wanted to show that the characteristics attributed to Woman Wisdom have been brought to fulfillment in Jesus. However, there is a significant difference between the two. Jesus was not only with God, "the Word *was* God." He was not only present at creation, "all things came to be through him." He not only dwelt among us, "the Word became flesh." The passage proceeds to develop other themes, such as light and faith. Pairing this reading with Sirach suggests that the primary theme today is wisdom.

This is the same gospel assigned for the third Mass on Christmas. On that day most people concentrate on the human nature of Jesus. On this Second Sunday after Christmas, we look again at his divine nature. Today we celebrate the cosmic Christ, God's incarnated gift, who comes to dwell in our midst. Just as Woman Wisdom was told by God to pitch her tent among the people, so the Divine Word has pitched a tent among us, bringing us the gift of salvation. With Paul we can cry out: "Blessed be the God and Father of our Lord Jesus Christ, who has blessed us in Christ with every spiritual blessing in the heavens, as he chose us in him, before the foundation of the world, to be holy and without blemish before him."

Praying with Scripture

- What gives meaning to your life? Why do you think that it does?

- How has Christ made a difference in your life?

- Make the responsorial psalm your prayer today.

EPIPHANY
Readings:
Isa 60:1–6; Ps 72:1–2, 7–8, 10–13;
Eph 3:2–3a, 5–6; Matt 2:1–12

WHERE DO YOU TURN ON THE LIGHT?

Although darkness can at times be very soothing, and even romantic, it can also be very dangerous and frightening. We can lose our way in the dark; we might bump into things and break them; we could fall and injure ourselves or others. When we are in the dark, we cannot perceive what or who might threaten our safety. The phrase *under the cover of darkness* suggests some dimension of deception, activity performed so that there is no detection. When we are in the dark and feel vulnerable, we instinctively reach out for the light switch.

The opposite of darkness is, of course, light. With it we are able to find our way; we can perceive rightly; we feel more secure. Scientific tests have shown that we may need darkness to sleep, but we need light to live. In many ways we are like the heliotropic plants that turn instinctively to the sun, not merely for warmth but also for life.

Darkness and light almost universally symbolize negative-positive polarity. In the first reading for today's feast, the prophet Isaiah uses the theme of darkness to refer to the gloomy plight of Israel as it seeks to recover from the exile, and that of light when he speaks about Israel's hope of future restoration. It should be noted that the light of which he speaks is no ordinary light. Rather, it is the glory of God that encircles the nation; it is a light so transforming that, in its turn, Israel will act as a light for others as well. This broken and decimated nation will radiate a brilliance that will guide others, and these others will come to Israel with their treasures. In this light there will be no fear, no deception, only the safety and blessing that God's graciousness can guarantee.

Epiphany means "manifestation." On this feast of the manifestation of God in the child Jesus, we celebrate the light that has come to lead us out of darkness. It is the glory of God that shines through the readings for today. The gospel tells us that this mystery was made known through a star, a wondrous phenomenon in the heavens, a light that pointed the way through darkness, at least for some. Was the star seen by just a few? Were the unassuming shepherds of Bethlehem and the studious Magi from the East the only ones who were granted sight of its splendor? Or might others have seen it, marveled at its brilliance, and then simply resumed the routine of their daily lives? Herod and the leaders in Jerusalem did not seem to know anything about the star. Is the manifestation of God reserved for only a select few? Who was to be illumined? Who was called out of darkness? For whom was the good news of Bethlehem meant?

According to Isaiah, the glory of God would shine first on Israel and then through Israel onto the other nations. The psalm response echoes this conviction. God's chosen one will "rule from sea to sea, / and from the River to the ends of the earth.... / All kings shall pay him homage, / all nations shall serve him." This same assertion is found in Paul's writings. According to him, the Gentiles are coheirs of this revelation. So, the manifestation of God is meant for all. However, we do not all receive it in the same way. The shepherds received it themselves, and then they announced it to others. The same was true with the Magi. They saw the star, and then announced its meaning to those they met in Jerusalem. Once they had found the child, however, they were told not to return to Jerusalem to provide more information about him. This detail reminds us that not everyone wants to live in the clarity of the light of God. Some do prefer the darkness of their own selfishness.

The Epiphany or feast of the Three Kings is not merely a time for the children to move some of the figurines in the Christmas crèche (if the crèche has even been kept up this long!). This is a very important feast in its own right. While the Western Church separates the commemorations of Christ's birth and his manifestation to the world, the Eastern Church still celebrates them together on this day. The West retains the connection of these two feasts by honoring the "twelve days of Christmas." However, even this tradition has lost much of its meaning and has survived simply as a delightful holiday song that has little religious meaning.

This feast is a clarion call for us. Just as ancient Israel was enlightened by the glory of God and then radiated that light to the rest of the world, just as the Magi from the east followed the star to the child and bravely proclaimed what they had found, so we have been called out of the darkness of our own complacency into the light of Christian witness. Today God is using us to turn the light on for others.

Praying with Scripture

- Pray for openness to God's light and for the courage to follow wherever it leads you.

- In what ways does your life give witness to your faith?

- Make the responsorial psalm your prayer today.

BAPTISM OF THE LORD
Readings:
Isa 42:1–4, 6–7; Ps 29:1–4, 9–10;
Acts 10:34–38; Mark 1:7–11

THROUGH THE WATERS TO NEW LIFE

The Christmas season closes with the feast of the Baptism of the Lord. Though it closes one door, it opens another, namely, a period of contemplation on the events of the public life of Jesus. The readings remind us that the one born of our flesh is the servant of God, the very Son of God, the one who brings a promise of justice and hope to a world in desperate need.

John's baptism "of repentance for the forgiveness of sins" (Mark 1:4) resembles a popular religious practice of ritual cleansing. It had symbolic inner value because of the cleansing properties of water. It obviously did not generate in Jesus what it might have generated in others, namely, remorse and the desire to reform one's life. We might wonder why the sinless Jesus would submit himself to this ritual. Commentators maintain that Jesus' baptism by John was for him a kind of ritual entry into his ministry. It provided him an occasion for divine affirmation of his messianic identity. This divine approval is trinitarian in character. The voice from heaven is a traditional ancient Israelite way of referring to divine communication. This divine voice identifies Jesus as "My beloved Son; with you I am well pleased." Finally, the Spirit descends upon him in the form of a dove.

John recognizes Jesus' superiority. Though John came before Jesus, he acknowledges that Jesus is: "One mightier than I....I am not worthy to stoop and loosen the thongs of his sandals." While John's baptism is a highly respected ritual of devotion, it is merely a baptism with water. On the other hand, Jesus will baptize with the Holy Spirit.

The gospel writer has taken great pains to show that the ministry of Jesus brings to fulfillment some of the expectations expressed in Isaiah. The mysterious individual found in the writings of that prophet is identified by God as "my servant whom I uphold, / my chosen one with whom I am pleased." The passage goes on to describe the manner of ministry the servant will undertake: "He shall bring forth justice to the nations... / open the eyes of the blind... / bring out prisoners from confinement." While he will be committed to a reform that will require assertiveness, he will still tenderly care for those who have been bruised by the vicissitudes of life. Finally, the servant will be able to accomplish these remarkable feats because the spirit of the Lord will be given to him. In other words, it will be the power of God working through the servant that will accomplish these things. This identification of Jesus with the servant of the Lord also throws light on aspects of Jesus' ministry. It will be a ministry of justice for all and of tenderness toward those who have been broken.

The story taken from Acts of the Apostles reinforces one theme from the gospel account and another from the reading from Isaiah. First, it mentions the baptism of Jesus and the bestowal upon him of the Holy Spirit and power. Second, in line with the responsibility of the servant to minister "to the nations," the disciples of Jesus widen the scope of their ministry to include the household of the Gentile Cornelius. These references to earlier traditions trace the progression of God's plan of salvation for all. It begins with the servant in Isaiah; next, it moves to Jesus, who brings that ministry to fulfillment; then, it prompts the followers of Jesus to continue his ministry. That same ministry, with the same divine approval, has now been given to us. Our own baptism brought us into the circle of the children of God and commissioned us to continue the work begun by Jesus. And what might this entail?

We live at a time of great unrest. Our world seems always poised on the brink of chaos; businesses and individuals face financial instability; the turmoil within the church threatens its long-standing trustworthiness. No one is untouched by some form of the chaos, which threatens to swallow us alive. Where can we turn when the institutions meant to be refuges from chaos are themselves the source of its threat?

In the Bible, chaos is frequently portrayed as unruly water threatening to wipe out every living thing (e.g., the flood in Genesis). Today's responsorial psalm reminds us in no uncertain terms: "The LORD is enthroned above the flood." It assures us that God rules over the chaos in which we find ourselves. Today's readings offer us direction as we struggle to deal with this turmoil. The response invites us to trust in God; Isaiah offers us a plan for restoring order; Acts challenges us to continue the work of Jesus. As he came forth from the waters of the Jordan, Jesus' life took a new direction; he was now prepared to take up his ministry. As his followers, we emerge from the waters of baptism as new people who, with God's help, are now fortified to encounter the chaos of our world. Today we do not look back to Christmas, but forward to the task ahead, trusting that some day it might be said of us: "Here is my servant whom I uphold."

Praying with Scripture

- Through whose voices have you heard God calling you in the past?

- In what ways might the ordinary things you do really be ministry?

- How might God be inviting you to reach out to others?

Lent

FIRST SUNDAY OF LENT
Readings:
Gen 9:8–15; Ps 25:4–9;
1 Pet 3:18–22; Mark 1:12–15

TAKE YOUR PLACES, PLEASE!

I never cease to be amazed at how much difficulty people have with the directive, "Take your places, please!" And it is not just children who cannot seem to follow it. Try to get graduate students to form a line for commencement. Many of our problems stem from our inability to know our place, or stay in our place. We disrespect national boundaries; we trespass on private property; we push our way to the front. This is often true in our relationships as well. We come uninvited to parties; we assume positions of superiority; we allow others to control us. We do not always know what places to take.

What does this have to do with Lent? Quite a bit. The first readings for all the Lenten Sundays celebrate God's various covenant relationships with us. We will see that the various covenants are marked by a rainbow, a test of faith, an inscription on stone tablets, the policy of a pagan king, receptive hearts, and, finally, a servant who speaks a word that rouses the weary. The relentless desire of God to be in relationship with us clearly comes forward in these readings.

We might say that Lent is a season of covenant making, and covenant marks our true place before God. Therefore, rather than simply enter into this season considering it merely as a penitential commemoration of the forty days that Jesus spent in the desert, let us view it from the perspective of our place in covenant relationship with God.

The first reading comes from the story of Noah, which is not merely a fanciful tale told to children. Nor is the bow in the sky simply a colorful sign that has been domesticated for greeting cards.

The ancient stories of creation frequently included some kind of cosmic battle fought between the forces of chaos and a youthful warrior god. Several Mesopotamian artifacts depict creator-gods with quivers full of arrows. For many ancient peoples, floodwaters symbolized what a mushroom cloud does for us today, namely, total annihilation.

In today's reading we see the cosmic order established by our mighty God after vanquishing the chaos that threatened the entire world. Hanging the bow in the sky is a sign that the primordial war is over, bow and arrows are no longer needed, and all of creation can rest secure. According to the biblical story, this is the first covenant made by God. It provides an overview of cosmic order, and it highlights the place of human beings within that order. This covenant is not made between God and Noah alone, but with Noah's descendants generation after generation. Nor is it merely made with humankind, but with all living creatures and with the earth itself. This covenant declares that God is in a providential relationship with all of natural creation, and will be so down through the ages.

And what is our place within this cosmic panorama? We are part of the breathless spectacle of life, along with every other living creature: the birds, the various tame and wild animals, the earth itself. However, because we do not know our place in this world, or are not willing to accept it, we often bring chaos back into it. We violate living systems; we horde natural resources; we fight wars over land or oil; we deprive each other of necessary food. We act as if the natural world is a personal commodity to do with as we please, and we use the fruits of this magnificent world as weapons against one another.

Lent is a time to put things back into order, to take our proper place in the world. To do this effectively, it might be good for us to spend some time in the desert, in some barren place devoid of excessive comforts and social distractions. We need not be frightened by what we find there. Though Jesus was tempted in the desert by Satan, he was comforted by God's angels. It may not be possible for us to go *out* to the desert, but we can all certainly go *in* to a deeper level of ourselves, to the inner conscience of which 1 Peter speaks.

Lent invites us to examine that conscience with honesty and new insight. It provides us with an opportunity to look anew at our place in this world as creatures of the earth, dependent upon it for sustenance and survival. We are reminded that our first responsibility is the nurture of life, not human life alone, but life itself. Our conscience alerts us to the fact that we cannot arrogantly march through the land, disdainful of it and of those others who live off its abundance. How can we genuinely renew our lives, if we overlook our fundamental groundedness in the cosmic covenant that is placed before us for our consideration this First Sunday of Lent?

Praying with Scripture

- In what ways do the forces of chaos have a hold on your life? In yourself; in your family; at your workplace; in the country; in the world?

- What role do natural elements play in this chaos?

- How might you work toward a change?

SECOND SUNDAY OF LENT
Readings:
Gen 22:1–2, 9a, 10–13, 15–18;
Ps 116:10, 15–19; Rom 8:31b–34;
Mark 9:2–10

DO YOU PROMISE?

Last Sunday we reflected on our covenant relationship with the created world. Today we consider the covenant promises made to Abraham. Though referred to as "The Sacrifice of Isaac," the story might be better named "The Testing of Abraham." The first line of the first reading identifies it as such. This is a troubling story. Having promised Abraham descendants and land, both necessary for that indistinguishable group to become a great nation, God asks him to sacrifice the very son through whom the promise was to be fulfilled. This would be not simply a personal tragedy, but the undoing of a nation yet to be realized. Just what is God doing? How trustworthy are God's promises?

During the recent past we have lost so many people of promise in whom we placed our hopes. They went to their offices or simply on a trip, and never returned home; they stood in defense of freedom, and never returned home. They soared among the stars, and never returned home. These were national and not simply personal tragedies. Just what is God doing? How trustworthy are the promises in which we hope?

What value can we find in such a troubling story as that of Abraham? What good can come from such disaster and heartache? The first reading sketches something of life itself. It highlights senseless, even cruel suffering. Though Isaac might be an innocent victim, he does not actually suffer. Abraham is the one put to the test, and from a human point of view, his response is terrifying. Perhaps there is another way to understand this test. Might it be that Abraham was asked to choose either the promises of God as they would be fulfilled in Isaac, or the very God who made the promises in the first place? Once again the story itself offers a clue. Abraham is told: "I know…how devoted you are to God." Without understanding how the promises will be fulfilled if Isaac is put to death, Abraham still trusts in God. We might ask: "Why should he and why should we trust a God who requires such great sacrifice?" The other readings for today answer this question.

Paul insists that, regardless of what we might have to endure in life, God's love for us cannot be questioned. He goes so far as to say that God's love is so great that, for our sake, not even Jesus was spared suffering. Some people may see God's willingness to sacrifice Jesus as simply another example of God's cruelty. But this would be wrong. Just as the first reading demonstrates that, out of devotion to God, Abraham is willing to sacrifice his greatest treasure, so, out of love for us, God is willing to sacrifice the greatest of all treasures.

The covenant that God made through Abraham was not for the sole advantage of Abraham's descendants, to hug it to their hearts in some exclusive way. Rather, the "chosen people," however that phrase is understood, were meant to be a source of blessing for all the nations of the world. This passage speaks of obedience, but the covenant to which it refers is grounded in faith. Without really understanding how God would fulfill the promise, Abraham believes in God. Here his faith or trust in God was tested, just as ours is, time and again.

God does not call us away from our dreams into a vacuum. If we are asked to relinquish a possible future, it is only so that we may be offered another possible future, God's future. Our aspirations may be noble, but the possibilities that God offers will outstrip them. Do we trust enough in God to believe this? Abraham was promised an heir; he relinquished his hold on his heir and he was granted heirs beyond counting. In the gospel, the disciples committed themselves to Jesus without realizing that he would allow himself to be handed over to death; he overwhelmed them when he was revealed as God's own beloved Son.

Such trust may sound good on paper, until we are confronted again with the bleeding wound left in our hearts when loved ones are ripped from our arms, or when dreams for the future are dashed for no apparent reason. Rather than think that God is playing some capricious game, we are summoned by today's readings to a different way of understanding, to the realization that the events of life are offering us a choice: Do we trust in promises as we perceive them, or do we trust in the God who makes promises that we may not comprehend?

While Lent can be rightly considered a time of testing, it is not a testing to see how much we can endure from or for God. Such a perception of God is found nowhere in the Bible. God's testing of us is really our opportunity to make a choice, as did Abraham.

Finally, the question of suffering in the world, particularly the suffering of the innocent, has always been problematic, and we have never been able to discover an adequate answer for it. Sometimes all we can really do is cry out with the psalmist: "I believed, even when I said, / 'I am greatly afflicted.'"

Praying with Scripture

- In the face of your deepest cares and greatest heartaches, remind yourself of God's tender love.

- Ask for the grace to trust in God despite what you may have to endure.

- Pray for those whose suffering has turned them away from God.

THIRD SUNDAY OF LENT
Readings:
Exod 20:1–17; Ps 19:8–11;
1 Cor 1:22–25; John 2:13–25

WORDS OF ETERNAL LIFE

(Today is the first of three Sundays set aside for the instruction of the catechumens who will be baptized on Holy Saturday. Referred to as *scrutinies,* these instructions are usually based on the gospel readings for Year A of the lectionary, not the readings assigned for today.)

On the first Sunday of Lent we reflected on the covenant that God made with the entire created world. Last week we pondered the covenant promises God made to Abraham and his descendants. Today we consider one aspect of yet a third covenant, that is, the law associated with the covenant God made through Moses.

The prominent television series *Law and Order* and other programs feature the courtroom as the stage upon which the human drama unfolds. This might suggest that we are grounded in principles of law. But are we? We still often applaud those who know how to get around the law. We don't seem as committed to law as a first impression might suggest.

The Hebrew word *torah* is usually translated as "law," but it might be better understood as "directive" or "instruction." The law stated in today's first reading and praised in the psalm response is not a burdensome yoke that weighs us down. Rather, it is a list of directives or instructions for living out our covenant relationship. In this sense the laws are truly words of eternal life.

Israel's law was not a set of rigid precepts. Again and again the psalm response depicts its life-enhancing attributes: It refreshes the soul and rejoices the heart; it is pure and true, more precious than gold. Ancient Israel considered the law a form of wisdom gained from reflection on life. This wisdom developed out of insights that demonstrated what will lead to happiness and what will not. The Israelites cherished the law much as the Greeks revered their philosophy. Today Paul uses these characterizations to make his point about the excellence of Christ.

It may be relatively easy to perceive the power of God in the miracles that Jesus performed, and we are not unlike those of whom Paul speaks, those who look for such signs. However, it takes faith to recognize the wisdom of God in Christ crucified. Yet this is precisely what Paul proclaims. From a human point of view, the image of Christ crucified may seem foolish, but it is far wiser than any human wisdom. But what does this mean? As the wisdom of God, Christ fulfills the expectations of any and all codes of law. In following him, we fulfill the requirements of the law; in following him, we live out our covenant relationship.

Jesus did not renounce the law; rather, he brought it to fulfillment. He showed us that external observance is not enough. He called for a commitment that is much deeper, a commitment that goes to the very heart of our covenant relationship with God. In the gospel reading we see that he *cleansed* the temple; he did not *violate* it, and many people grasped the meaning of his actions; "they saw the signs he was doing."

Jesus' actions were acted-out prophecy and his words were prophetic foretelling. By driving the merchants out of the temple precincts, he symbolically cleansed it of superficial, external practice. Identifying God as his Father, he affirmed his right to act in this bold manner. The future events of his death and resurrection would be the ultimate signs of his authority, but it would take faith, both then and now, to recognize this.

How does this touch us today? Lent is a time of personal scrutiny, a time to look deeply at our covenant commitment as expressed through our attitude toward the law. We, and the catechumens with us, learn the *torah* requirements as the basis of our covenant responsibilities. But there is more; we have the example of Jesus to demonstrate how these responsibilities might actually be lived out.

Filled with zeal for the house of God, that special place where humans and God meet, Jesus challenges religious practice that is simply external. It is important to note that the Greek word for *house, oîkos,* can also mean *household.* In fact, this latter meaning is probably what was intended in the original biblical saying, "Zeal for your house[hold] consumes me" (Ps 69:10). This rendering of the word raises a serious challenge for us. How zealous are we for the household of God? How committed are we to the people who make up the church, not merely those whom we find in the external building, but all those who are in any way part of the people of God?

We may recognize a connection between this zeal and the directives we find in the covenant law. While these precepts provide a sketch of our responsibilities toward God, there is also an obvious social dimension to most of them. They outline the way we are to live with and respect each other. Commitment to the deeper meaning of these laws is the way we are called to be faithful to our covenant with God.

Praying with Scripture

- What is your attitude toward the law of God? How meaningful is it in your life?

- Choose a particular Lenten practice. Why is it observed? What is its deep religious meaning?

- Are you consumed with zeal for the household of God? If not, in what ways might you change this?

FOURTH SUNDAY OF LENT
Readings:
2 Chr 36:14–16, 19–23; Ps 137:1–6;
Eph 2:4–10; John 3:14–21

HOW DO I LOVE THEE?

How do I love thee? Let me count the ways.
I love thee to the depth and breadth and height

my soul can reach when feeling out of sight
for the ends of being and ideal grace.

Such tender words of the poet Elizabeth Barrett Browning (*Sonnets from the Portuguese*, XLIII) reflect a bit of the all-encompassing character of human love. Still, human love is only a reflection of divine love and somehow participates in it. For this reason, these words could well be placed in the mouth of God this Sunday, for all three readings illustrate God's merciful love.

The first reading opens with a dispassionate chronicling of the people's willful violation of their covenant relationship with God. It tells how, in response to their callous behavior, God allowed their enemies to triumph over them. But this was not the end for them. Once they had repented—and in moving words the psalm response has captured their sentiments of repentance—God allowed them to return. Their return (return and repent come from the same Hebrew word) is first a return to God and then a return to Jerusalem, where they might live a life dedicated to God.

The extent of God's love is recounted in the gospel. There we read that the only son of God was sent into the world in order to save it. In John's gospel "the world" frequently refers to that dimension of human life that is antagonistic toward the things of God. That is not the meaning here. Rather, the writer insists that God loves the world, seeks to draw people out of darkness into light, and does whatever is necessary to save them from their own sinfulness.

Paul reiterates this teaching about divine love in the reading from Ephesians. He declares that God saves us through Christ. But why should God do this? Certainly not because we deserve it. In fact, Paul claims that God saved us while we were still in our transgressions or mired in our sinfulness. God saves us out of mercy, that covenant characteristic known in the Hebrew tradition as loving-kindness or steadfast love. God's merciful love alone marks the "ends of being and ideal grace," to use Browning's words.

During the first three weeks of Lent we considered various aspects of our covenant relationship with God and the privileges and responsibilities that flow from it. Today we turn our gaze onto God's covenant relationship with us, and we are astounded at what we perceive. Despite our infidelity, God remains faithful to us; despite the steps we take toward our own destruction, God continues to offer us a second chance at life. Such are the "depth and breadth and height" of God's love.

However, and it is a significant however, God does not force anything upon us. We are free to choose. We can accept God's loving gestures, or we can refuse them. We see this in today's readings. Before the Israelites could return to the land, they had to return to God; in the gospel account, Nicodemus was told that people can choose to believe or not believe in Christ; they can prefer darkness to the light. There has always been a choice. Today the choice is ours to make. Will we make it? Very few of us explicitly choose against God, but can we honestly absolve ourselves of actions that resemble those described in the first reading? Haven't we, today's political leaders, religious leaders, or ordinary people, sometimes "added infidelity to infidelity"? Do we heed the warnings of God's messengers, or do we scoff at them, even silence them? Are we not sometimes so entrenched in our own transgressions that we do not see how the consequences of our arrogance may cause our world to fall down upon us?

If we are honest we must admit that this has indeed been the case in our personal lives; lately we recognize that it has happened in our church; it has certainly been the situation in our country and in the broader world. This may have been the case in the past, and perhaps even in the present, but what about the future? We are not bound to perpetuate such deplorable situations. We are able to make new choices. So—what will we choose?

Despite this focus on our own sinfulness and the dire consequences that flow from it, the predominant theme for this Sunday is divine mercy. However, we can only comprehend its magnanimous character and boundless scope if we see it in relation to our own culpability. As the readings show us how important it is to acknowledge our guilt and to return to God, they concentrate on God's eagerness to enfold us in the warm embrace of divine mercy.

Confident in God's merciful love, we are able to repent, return to God, and start anew. Like the people of ancient Israel, we can indeed rebuild our broken lives and our disgraced church.

We can create a world based on cooperation rather than competition, on respect rather than discrimination. God's love has been offered; the choice is ours.

Praying with Scripture

- In what ways have the crises in your life, in the church, in the country, or in the world in any way undermined your belief in God's merciful love?

- Realistically, what can you do to resolve such crises?

- How might renewed confidence in God's love change your thinking and your actions?

FIFTH SUNDAY OF LENT
Readings: *Jer 31:31–34; Ps 51:3–4, 12–15;*
Heb 5:7–9; John 12:20–33

"THE HOUR HAS COME"

The season of Lent is drawing to its conclusion. The hour has come. We may think that the hour referred to in John's gospel is the hour of Jesus' death. It is, but the author gives that dreaded hour a most unexpected meaning. He claims that the hour of Jesus' death is really the hour of his glorification. He further insists that Jesus is glorified, not as a martyr, but as the source of new life for us. We hear this so often that we might fail to realize the paradox here: Jesus' death brings us new life. What does this mean? The readings for today provide us with an answer.

Through the prophet Jeremiah, God announces a new covenant. This does not mean that the other covenants have been abrogated. We are still creatures of the earth (Gen 9), who cling to God's promises (Gen 22), who are subject to God's law (Exod 20), and who are embraced by God's mercy (Jer 31). This new covenant will be something quite different, something extraordinary. Written on our hearts, it will effect an interior transformation.

The evils of today, those we witness and those of which we are a part, require much more than simple external change. If we are honest, we will admit that we need radical interior transformation. Our self-absorption and unbridled pursuit of personal satisfaction, our arrogant sense of superiority, the hatred and revenge that eat at our hearts, can be remedied only at their roots. We are certainly in need of a new covenant commitment.

The technical covenant formula, "I will be their God, and they shall be my people," is comparable to the marriage formula: "I do take you as my spouse." This language bespeaks loving intimacy. These words should make us step back in total amazement, for they imply that in the face of human infidelity, God establishes a covenant of the heart. Perhaps the failure of so many human commitments between couples, within families, at the workplace, and even among nations, clouds our eyes to the reality of God's unbounded love. This is a remarkable covenant. When will it be established? "The days are coming, says the LORD."

The sentiments of Psalm 51 might well be our response to God's astounding offer of loving commitment: "Have mercy on me... / wipe out my offense... / A clean heart create for me." Today we might say: "Help me to accept what I find bothersome in others; heal me of my stubbornness, my selfishness, and my pride; cleanse me of hatred of people of cultures that are foreign to me and of nations that might pose a threat." God announces that the days are coming when all of this will happen. Deep down in our hearts, can we believe this? Are we doing anything to bring it about? Yet even in the face of such doubt, God declares: "The days are coming."

As we turn to the gospel, we hear Jesus say, "The hour has come." True, it is the hour of his death, but it is also the hour of his glorification. While this glorification may refer in part to the unique relationship that he enjoys with God ("a voice came from heaven"), the reading suggests that it also has something to do with the new life that will spring from his death. Jesus' obedience to his destiny, mentioned in both the gospel and the reading from Hebrews, opens the doors of life for us. In this he is glorified.

To whom will this new life be offered? The words in Jeremiah are addressed to both Israel and Judah, the two kingdoms that made up the entire nation. God calls these separated people to "be my people." The gospel teaches us that this new covenant is not merely meant for the Jewish people. Greeks, representatives of the entire world, came to see Jesus. In other words, all women and men of integrity are to be invited to this covenant. Jesus declares: "I will draw everyone to myself."

Today we hear of a new covenant, a clean heart, a grain of wheat pregnant with fruitfulness. These are all poetic ways of describing the new way of living into which we can step if we so choose. The disarray of so much of our lives makes us realize that we must choose a different way of living. However, radical transformation does not come without a price. For our sake, Jesus suffered dearly, and he insists: "Whoever serves me must follow me." And there is the rub!

Now that our Lenten journey is almost over, what have we learned from the readings of this season? In what ways are we willing to change? Whom are we willing to help or to forgive? To what extent are we willing to die to our own selfishness so that the fruits of the new covenant can be brought forward? The hour of decision has come.

Praying with Scripture

- Read the psalm response prayerfully, asking God for a clean heart and a steadfast spirit.

- Choose one or two ways in which you can live a renewed life.

- Pray for the grace to be faithful to your new insights, regardless of the price they may exact.

PALM SUNDAY OF THE LORD'S PASSION

Readings:
Isa 50:4–7; Ps 22:8–9, 17–20, 23–24;
Phil 2:6–11; Mark 14:1—15:47

DID YOU KNOW THAT YOU'RE MY HERO?

When I was a child, I climbed up on a billboard in order to catch a glimpse of a war hero who had returned from an unpopular military assignment. We waved flags and cheered and threw confetti, despite the fact that this hero had come home this time in disgrace. It was thrilling! I was proud that I could say: I was there; I saw him, the one about whom I had heard stories of such marvelous feats. I wonder what the people of Bethphage and Bethany thought as Jesus processed toward Jerusalem. Had they been as excited as I was? It seems, however, that their enthusiasm would quickly turn to disdain when he was captured, tried, and put to death. Hero worship does not seem to enjoy a long shelf life.

We don't usually think of Jesus as a hero, but hero he is. He is our savior, the one who handed himself over for our sake, the one who was abandoned so that we might belong. Today when the excitement of the parade is over and the waving of the palms ceases, we should spend some time reflecting on the character of our hero. On this first day of Holy Week, we should try to understand why a week of betrayal and denial, of mockery and bloodshed is called holy.

Today's readings paint pictures of terror and viciousness. Isaiah speaks of a beating and derision; the psalmist staggers under the burden of abandonment and assault; the gospel describes each excruciating episode of Jesus' passion. How can such horrors be endured? But they are endured. In fact, for some incomprehensible reason, they appear to be embraced. Trusting in God, the Isaian hero offered himself to his persecutors, some inner certainty convincing him that he was not disgraced. With lyricism heard through the ages, Paul proclaims that Jesus, our hero, emptied himself and humbly accepted death on the cross. Anticipating his torment, Jesus declares: "Not what I will but what you will." What is it that empowers people to face unthinkable suffering bravely and unflinchingly? There is only one reason, and it is unconditional love.

Traditionally during Holy Week, we focus on the sufferings of Jesus. However, it is not suffering, not even the suffering of Jesus, that makes this week holy. Rather, it is holy because of the inexplicable and immeasurable love that prompted that suffering. Genuine love often empowers, even transforms us. We know that love of family can engender unselfishness, and love of country can inspire heroism. This week we see that, driven by love for all, Jesus willingly accepted the consequences of his messianic role.

Today's readings, like the events of this week, begin with excitement that is electric and acclaim that is unabashed, but they end in numbing devastation and a sense of emptiness. It is too easy to say that the people were fickle, one moment supporting Jesus and the next rejecting him. It was probably more a case of frustrated expectations. They cheered him as the son of David, and when he failed to act like a conquering king, they turned their backs on him and looked for another. This kind of behavior is not difficult to understand, because, unfortunately, we too give up on people when they do not meet our expectations.

This week is holy because of love, but it is love misunderstood. Jesus is a hero, but not in the traditional pattern of heroism. He actually looks more like a victim. He is not triumphant, as we understand triumph. Instead, he appears to be a failure. Judging by one set of standards, standards not unlike those of many people of his day, he has not met our expectations either. But according to another standard, the standard of unconditional love, he has far surpassed all of our expectations.

Parents, lovers, patriots, committed people of every kind often disregard their own desires and comfort for the sake of those they love. Are they heroes? Of course they are! Are they failures? Certainly not! Have they frustrated our expectations? Quite the contrary. We may even expect them to act out of such personal disregard. Human sacrifice like this gives us an insight into the meaning of the sacrifice of Jesus. The love that prompts us to give of ourselves is but a reflection of the magnanimous love of God which, in the guise of suffering and death, unfolds before us this week.

The conditions of our world may make us feel that this is a terrible week, not a holy one. However, we can change this, if only in some small way. We will make it holy if we can begin to realize the depth of God's magnanimous love. We will make it holy if we can bring unconditional love into the lives of those around us. We will make it holy if we live according to the paradoxical standards of Jesus who, though publicly disgraced, is still our hero.

Praying with Scripture

- Reflect on the times when God's unconditional love has been mediated to you through others.

- Where in your life might God be calling you to love others unconditionally?

- How might you alleviate the suffering of Jesus that continues in the lives of others?

Easter Season

EASTER (B)
Readings:
Acts 10:34a, 37–43; Ps 118:1–2, 16–17, 22–23;
Col 3:1–4 (or 1 Cor 5:6b–8); John 20:1–9

Alleluia!

One of the most impressive scenes in the movie *The Wizard of Oz* is the one that depicts Dorothy's entrance into the Emerald City. When she opens the door of her Kansas home, thinking that she will see her aunt and uncle's familiar farmyard, the original sepia tones of the film are converted into brilliant Technicolor. The tornado-beaten earth gives way to a boldly colorful magical land, where everything is strange but radiantly beautiful. I am reminded of this scene as I reflect on the even more powerful transformation that we celebrate at Easter. In a way similar to but far surpassing that scene from the movie, a wondrous world of mystery opens up before us, inviting us to step into it.

The movies are not the only medium that reenacts transformation. The thread of dramatic transformation in the form of reversal is woven throughout the readings of the Easter Vigil. They lead us through the chaotic waters of creation over the rainbow to the saving waters of baptism; they carry us safely through the threatening Red Sea and the frightening wilderness to a place of hope and promise. Leading us through muted sepia colors, they bring us to the threshold of a spectacular vista more glorious than the Emerald City. This vista is not a fanciful dream, as was Dorothy's. It is real, as real as life and death. Actually, it is as real as death and new life.

Our first step out of the sepia world of the past into the glittering world of Easter mystery is really a step into the waters of baptism. The Vigil readings prepare us for that climactic moment when either we make our initial plunge into these saving waters or we renew the baptismal commitment we have already made. The words we pronounce are simple: "I do believe! I do renounce!" But as is the case in every covenant commitment, these words are themselves transformative; they recreate us as new people.

The gospel readings for both the Easter Vigil and the Mass of Easter Day report the utter confusion of Jesus' followers. The women who rose early in the morning did not go to rejoice in the resurrection of their Lord. They went to anoint a dead body. Confronted by the empty tomb, not even Mary, one of his closest followers, imagined that he had risen. Rather, she concluded that Jesus' body had been taken away. Peter and John rushed to the empty tomb, but they did not understand what had happened either. Despite what Jesus had told them before his death, no one seemed to have expected anything like a resurrection. But then, who could blame them? The resurrection was a unique manifestation of the mysterious power of God, not some imaginative MGM production.

The gospels do not describe what happened to Jesus at the moment of resurrection. In fact, all of the Easter readings focus on the implications of the resurrection in the lives of Jesus' followers. Paul instructs his converts that, joined to Christ, they must now live a new way. Having been raised with Christ from the dead, they must purge themselves of their old ways of living. They are on the threshold of newness. A wondrous world of mystery has opened up before them, inviting them to step into it.

We are not unlike those first followers. Though we know well the Easter story, we never seem fully to grasp its meaning. Like them, we so often continue to live burdened with our dashed hopes and with our misunderstanding of God's mysterious power. Like them, we come to the tomb and expect to find death, but instead we find signs of a new life that we cannot even begin to comprehend. Like them, we do not realize that our history has been broken open and is now filled with the presence of the resurrected Christ.

Unfortunately, the transformation of which the readings speak is not easily recognized. Our world overwhelms us with evidence of death and destruction and not with signs of the lavish life of the Emerald City. Despite this, our faith assures us that the tomb is empty because Jesus has risen; it assures us that death has been swallowed up by life. Only with faith can we accept this mystery. However, if we do accept it, and live our lives believing that this has indeed happened, we will make it real in our world.

Paul tells us how to do this. We must purge ourselves of malice and wickedness, of resentfulness and revenge. We must refrain from taking delight in the misfortunes of others and from taking advantage of them for our own benefit. Instead we must live in sincerity and truth, neighborliness and honesty. Easter is a time to celebrate life, to value life in all of its forms and at all of its stages. A wondrous world of mystery has opened up before us, inviting us to step into it. This is why we cry out: "Alleluia!"

Praying with Scripture

- In what ways is Easter faith calling you to a new life?

- What holds you back from stepping across the threshold into resurrection-living?

- Pray for the courage to take the step.

SECOND SUNDAY OF EASTER
Readings:
*Acts 4:32–35; Ps 118:2–4, 13–15, 22–24;
1 John 5:1–6; John 20:19–31*

"WE HAVE SEEN THE LORD!"

"We have seen the Lord!" Who has not longed to hear those words? Or who has not longed for the experience that gave birth to the words? So many of us are like Thomas in today's gospel. Not that we are doubters, but that our faith is based on the words of others. Someone else has the experience, and we hear about it from that person. We are like Thomas because we want experience, not hearsay.

But that is not exactly true. God does not favor a chosen few with an experience of the Risen Christ and then require the rest of us simply to take it on their word. Not at all! The resurrection means that Jesus is alive for each of us. At the end of his book *Life of Jesus,* François Mauriac reminds us that since the resurrection we are apt to encounter the Lord when and where we least expect. Today's readings provide us with a few examples of such unexpected meetings.

The description of the early Christian community found in Acts reminds us that Christ is indeed among us, living within the community of believers, in the members of his body. He is alive in those who are one in heart and mind, who share what they have with each other. These early Easter-people were so transformed by their resurrection experience that nonbelievers stood in wonder at them and exclaimed: "These Christians, see how they love one another!"

We are no different! We too find Christ in our community. His vulnerability can be found in the children and in the elderly; his courage is in those who stand bravely for principle or who accept suffering with dignity; his kindness shines forth in the smiles of others; his healing power is in their gentle touch.

We also meet him in the weaker members of his body. Jesus invited Thomas to touch his wounds. He extends that same invitation to us. It is his fear that we see in the eyes of the mentally ill; it is his terror that grips the refugee or victim of war; his need reaches out to us in those who are lost, hungry, or imprisoned. As Mauriac reminds us, this Risen Christ might be just around the corner, often unseen if we lack eyes of faith. Have we experienced this mysterious Christ? Can our contemporaries say of us: "These Christians, see how they love one another"?

"On the evening of that first day of the week," Jesus granted his disciples the power to forgive sins. It might seem strange that he chose that day to bestow this power, but the time was well chosen. Just as through the resurrection we step into a new transformed life, so by means of forgiveness we enter transformed into a new life.

Forgiveness may be as difficult to understand as it is to practice. The cliché "forgive and forget" is misleading. We are not really expected to forget, to overlook offenses as if they had never happened. That would be naive, and it might suggest that sinning against another is not really an important matter. Genuine forgiveness acknowledges that sin, particularly serious sin, has been committed. It may also demand that punishment, even severe punishment, be exacted. However, it does not condemn the offender to a lifetime of guilt. It believes in transformation. In fact, the act of forgiveness can itself be transformative.

Jesus extended his forgiving peace to his disciples and then gave them the power to extend that same forgiving peace to others. This scene is traditionally associated with the sacrament of penance. However, forgiveness can be granted many different ways. The troubling times in which we live remind us that we are all in need of forgiveness. Many of us are either perpetrators of some offense against another or we harbor resentment and animosity toward the offender. Before we can begin anew we need to forgive or to be forgiven.

There might even be times when, like Thomas, we have to forgive ourselves. I was struck by the comment of a father whose son was fighting in Iraq. When asked by a reporter for what he prayed, he responded: "I pray that whatever he has to do, my son can live with himself when it's all over."

"On the evening of that first day of the week," Jesus transformed into a sacramental rite the very human experience of forgiving, thereby assuring us that we too can act in this way through his power. Whether the circumstances are trivial or heroic, whether the forgiveness is extended or received, in situations where there has been an offense, we do indeed encounter the Risen Lord.

Reflection on today's readings reminds us that the world is charged with the glory of the resurrection. What we need are open eyes that can recognize the Risen Lord in our midst and willing hearts that will enable others to encounter Christ through us. Only then will we be able to proclaim: "We have seen the Lord!"

Praying with Scripture

- Where in your life have you encountered the Risen Lord? In what kind of situations might you have failed to see him?

- What can you do so that others will encounter Christ through you?

- Make every effort this week to forgive at least one person.

THIRD SUNDAY OF EASTER
Readings:
Acts 3:13–15, 17–19; Ps 4:2, 4, 7–9;
1 John 2:1–5a; Luke 24:35–48

"HAVE YOU ANYTHING HERE TO EAT?"

The gospels are filled with stories about Jesus sharing a meal. Some of them illustrate his observance of feasts such as Passover (Luke 17:35); others depict him as a dinner guest at the homes of Simon the Pharisee (Luke 7:36) or Jesus' friend Martha (Luke 10:40). There is even mention that Jesus was criticized for eating so often and not fasting as did the ascetic John the Baptist. Today's gospel opens with a report delivered by two disciples. They had journeyed with Jesus, conversing with him along the way, yet recognizing him only "in the breaking of the bread." Since this phrase was a standard Christian reference to the Eucharist, it is clear that what the disciples thought was a customary sharing of food was changed by Jesus into a sacramental meal. They now realized that what they thought was a simple offering to a stranger introduced them to a profound religious experience.

The two disciples had not even finished describing their experience when Jesus stood in the midst of the group. "They were startled and terrified." Why? Because Jesus, who had died, was now among them, alive. The gospel paints a tender scene. Jesus first comforted his disciples with words of peace and reassurance. Then, in order to prove that he was not a ghost but a real living person, he asked them for something to eat. Like so many other "appearance" stories, this account lays bare the incredulity of the disciples. It shows that they had little comprehension of who Jesus was and what he had undergone. And so "he opened their minds to understand the Scriptures," explaining how he had brought many of its cherished passages to fulfillment. In doing so, he gave them more than bread to chew on.

Jesus was not only the center of their amazement, but he was also the focus of their instruction. Like a patient teacher, he went over once again the lessons he had taught them earlier during his public ministry, the meaning of which they obviously had not grasped at the time. Now, in the light of the resurrection, he explained how he had truly fulfilled the aspirations of Israel, even though he had fulfilled them in a way that the people could never have imagined. Now, through the very simple human acts of breaking bread and eating fish, he opened their inner eyes, enabling them to see that it really was he.

Later, as the first reading shows, Peter turned to the same sacred tradition and delivered a commanding lesson on messianic fulfillment. He placed Jesus squarely within the tradition of the ancestors Abraham, Isaac, and Jacob. In this way he also linked the tradition of ancient Israel with the newly formed Christian community. In his instruction to the people, he acknowledged that their leaders, and the people themselves, acted out of ignorance when they rejected Jesus and put him to death for making the claims that he did. Peter knew from his own experience that it was only after the resurrection that one came to realize that the claims were valid; Jesus is indeed the Holy and Righteous One.

The passage from the Letter to John provides yet another dimension to this portrait of Jesus. Not only is he the fulfillment of the ancient traditions of Israel, the Holy and Righteous One raised from the dead by God, but he is also our Advocate with God. In a bold statement, the author claims: "He is expiation for our sins." This phrase identifies the execution of Jesus as a ritual sacrifice. This language suggests that Jesus fulfilled the role of the scapegoat, the unfortunate creature that was driven out of the camp into the wilderness with the sins of the people on its back (Lev 16:10). By means of this ancient ceremony, the price was paid for the transgressions of the people, yet the people themselves were spared. This theological tradition lies behind Jesus' own teaching when, in the gospel, he refers to "repentance, for the forgiveness of sins."

It is easy to identify with the disciples in their fear and lack of understanding. Since they offered him baked fish to eat, one might conclude that they had returned to their previous occupations and had resumed their former lives. Why shouldn't they? It did not look as if he had changed anything. The power structures of Imperial Rome and of the synagogue still held sway over the people. Any religious enthusiasm that he had engendered had dissipated with his death. Even the few faithful disciples were now living with disillusionment and a sense of profound loss. What else were they to do?

We too get so caught up in the details of everyday life that we fail to recognize the Risen Lord in our midst. We look for extraordinary events rather than for the extraordinary within ordinary events. All we can do is go on with our lives, believing that he is indeed in our midst, hoping that someday we too will recognize him "in the breaking of the bread," or hear the simple words: "Have you anything here to eat?"

Praying with Scripture

- Pray for the grace to have your inner eyes opened so that you might recognize the Risen Christ in our midst.

- Develop the habit of spending a short period of time each day prayerfully meditating on the scriptures.

- How might you make your ordinary meals "sacramental"?

FOURTH SUNDAY OF EASTER
Readings:
Acts 4:8–12; Ps 118:1, 8–9, 21–23, 26, 28–29; 1 John 3:1–2; John 10:11–18

I'll Take Care of It!

Today is traditionally known as Good Shepherd Sunday. For many of us, mention of sheep conjures up the image of a warm coat or the memory of a good meal. We may remember the nursery rhyme *Mary Had a Little Lamb,* or the hand puppet made from a sock named Lamb Chop, but very few of us regard sheep as familiar companions. Thus we might not appreciate the depths of intimacy captured in the declaration: "I am the good shepherd."

For many people in the ancient world, shepherding was more than an occupation; it was their avenue of survival, their life, and their very identity. The life of shepherds was anything but carefree. The needs of their sheep determined how they spent their time, for their flocks had to be fed, watered, and protected. Because of the total commitment of the shepherd to the sheep, this image seemed an appropriate one to characterize the king, who was also expected to be totally committed to his people. It was because these human leaders failed in their responsibilities toward their charges that God declared: "I myself will look after and tend my sheep" (Ezek 34:11).

The gospel description of the good shepherd matches perfectly the responsibilities of both the sheepherder and the king. The introductory words of Jesus' declaration, "I am" *(egō eimi),* are reminiscent of God's response to Moses when he asked for God's name: "I am who I am" (Exod 3:14). Is Jesus claiming to be divine by making the words "I am" his own? Is he assuming guardianship responsibilities over the people? The answer to both questions is a subtle but unmistakable "yes." The gospel account is very clear on this matter. Jesus describes himself as a conscientious shepherd who is willing to protect his flock even to the point of risking his own life for them. Ravenous animals were extremely dangerous when their frantic need for survival drove them to be particularly ferocious. Add to this the fact that shepherds usually had only a staff and nearby stones to ward off such animals, and one begins to see that shepherding was a perilous occupation, not a peaceful one with abundant time for contemplative reverie.

The gospel's depiction of Jesus as a good shepherd adds a very significant feature to this traditional pastoral picture. Traditionally, there were shepherds for the various flocks. Jesus claims that he is attentive not only to the needs of his own flock, but to those sheep of other flocks as well. In other words, his guardianship is universal. Actually, if there is only one good shepherd, logically, there is really only one flock. This appears to be the way Jesus envisioned the situation: "There will be one flock, one shepherd."

This is all very poetic, but how does it relate to people who live in a technological society rather than in the hills and plains of ancient Israel, people who are struggling with the realities of war and deprivation? Today's readings encourage us in our need to turn to this "good shepherd" whose primary concern is our safety and well-being. The world in which we all live is very dangerous. War is always being waged somewhere; people are displaced; families are torn apart; and terrorism runs rampant. Hatred and revenge consume the hearts of many; violence destroys all hope; and millions of women, men, and children struggle for mere survival. We are in desperate need of some kind of shepherd. If there is to be but one flock and one shepherd, however, then we and those with whom we might be at odds all belong to the same community with the same unselfish guardian.

The first reading reports that Peter, filled with the Holy Spirit, boldly proclaimed that even the name of Jesus was able to accomplish great feats. Jesus was not a mighty warrior who came in military array. Rather, he was rejected, hunted down, humiliated, tortured, and hung naked on a tree to die in shame. He thus became the cornerstone of the building, holding it together, forming a firm foundation so that the structure would not collapse. Jesus our shepherd is an unlikely savior, if we are expecting extraordinary, aggressive behavior. This is not to say that he is without power. On the contrary, his powerlessness was his own choosing: "I lay down my life in order to take it up again." His strength was in his willingness to forego the use of military strength and, instead, to call upon moral strength, to offer himself for the sake of others.

Here again we see that Easter has turned things inside out and upside down. Life springs from death; strength is born of weakness; fulfillment is found in unselfishness. These words may sound empty in times of war, violence, and hatred, but they cry out the truth of the resurrection. We may feel helpless in the face of the terrors unleashed in today's world, but the words of Jesus should comfort us: "I am the good shepherd." And what might these words mean today? Turn to me; trust in me; I'll take care of it.

Praying with Scripture

- Call on the "good shepherd" to lead you out of the valley of death into the new life of resurrection.

- Is there anything in your life that might be threatening the safety of the flock?

- Pray for the grace to open your heart to the "other sheep" as Jesus has.

FIFTH SUNDAY OF EASTER
Readings:
Acts 9:26–31; Ps 22:26–28, 30–32;
1 John 3:18–24; John 15:1–8

IN THE ASSEMBLY OF THE PEOPLE

The tragedy of Philip Nolan, the major character in the story "The Man Without a Country," was not merely that he was forbidden ever again to set foot on U.S. soil or even hear spoken the name of his country of origin. His fate, chosen by the man himself in a moment of anger, meant that he did not belong to a nation of people anymore. He was literally a man without a community. At first he might have been satisfied with his impulsive decision. But soon he came to realize what we eventually all realize, namely, that as independent as we like to think we are, as human beings we desperately need to belong. Today's readings form a kind of triptych, a three-part illustration depicting what it means to belong to a postresurrection community.

The first panel (the reading from Acts) is quite realistic in its presentation. It shows Paul, shortly after his conversion, arriving in Jerusalem with Barnabas. While Paul may have been eager to join the group of disciples, they were understandably suspicious of him. After all, not too long ago he had diligently searched for them in order to hand them over to the Jewish authorities intent on stamping out this new religious movement. On the word of Barnabas, the Christians accepted him into their number and eventually even protected him when his life was in jeopardy.

This is a remarkable community. They not only forgave their former persecutor, but they actually embraced him as a new member. How many communities today exercise such a sense of reconciliation? How many communities open their hearts and their doors to people whose sins have become public? Jesus did not hold Paul's sin against him and so, following this example, neither did his followers. This accepting attitude is evidence of the presence of the Risen Lord in the postresurrection community.

The exhortation found in the second panel (the first Letter of John) alerts us to the twofold bond that unites all members of this community. We are told to "believe in the name of [God's] Son, Jesus Christ, and [to] love one another." This love of others is not based on personal preference any more than the acceptance of Paul was based on it. Rather, everything is based on faith in the Risen Lord. We first believe in the Risen Lord, and then this faith manifests itself in love of others.

The love to which John calls us is neither easy nor romantic. It is not love merely "in word or speech but in deed and truth." It manifests itself in ways that might call for a kind of heroism. This heroism might include accepting back those who earlier had turned away; or it could require that we be open to those who live their lives in ways that we consider unorthodox; or perhaps it calls us to welcome the stranger or those who are in any way threatened. Such love, which is inspired by the Spirit, is evidence of the presence of the Risen Lord in the postresurrection community.

Jesus' declaration to his disciples (John's Gospel) constitutes the center panel, and is really the focal point of the triptych. While the first two panels emphasize the bond that unites members of the community with each other, this centerpiece highlights the union of the members with Jesus himself. The metaphor of vine and branches, a metaphor that under the circumstances is quite bold, vividly characterizes the intimate nature of the relationship existing between Jesus and his followers. A vine is made up of its branches, and the life of the vine is the life of the branches. Jesus lives in his branches, and his branches live in his life. The vine bears fruit through its branches, and the branches bear the fruit of the vine. As important as the branches are, the vine is not totally dependent on any one branch or group of branches. However, there is no vine if there are no branches at all. In such a case, there is only a trunk, and that is not the metaphor that Jesus uses here.

In the face of possible pruning, Jesus declares: "Remain in me, as I remain in you." Don't separate yourself from me; don't try to make it on your own; don't renounce your membership in me. You are not without a country; you are not without a community; you are not without a source of life. We are branches of the true vine, joined to the vine and through the vine to each other. If the life of Jesus flows through our "veins," we will "bear much fruit." We will indeed shine forth in our world as a community called together and enlivened by the power of the resurrection. We will be a reconciling community, open to others and able to show the world that reconciliation with our enemies is possible. We will be a community bound to each other by love and able to bring genuine love to a world eaten away by hatred. We ourselves will be the evidence of the presence of the Risen Lord in the postresurrection community.

Praying with Scripture

- Where in your community is there a need for reconciliation? What can you do to accomplish it?

- In what ways might genuine love transform or heal your community?

- Spend time reflecting on your intimate union with Jesus.

SIXTH SUNDAY OF EASTER
Readings:
Acts 10:25–26, 34–35, 44–48; Ps 98:1–4;
1 John 4:7–10; John 15:9–17

WHAT'S LOVE GOT TO DO WITH IT?

Jesus' command to love is found in his Last Supper discourse as reported in John's Gospel. This exhortation is considered the heart of Jesus' teaching. This is certainly true with regard to the portrait of Jesus as found in John's Gospel. There we see that love for others is grounded in God's love for Jesus and Jesus' resulting love for us. This is a profound message, one that we have heard again and again. It may be so familiar to us that we slip over its obvious meaning without considering some of its most challenging implications.

It is probably difficult for many of us to grasp the meaning of God's love for Jesus. The gospels do not always help us in this matter either. Though Jesus consistently spoke of his intimate relationship with the one he called Father, this relationship did not protect him from the misunderstanding of others, their hatred of him, and his ultimate suffering and death at their hands. This does not mean that God did not love Jesus. Rather, it means that the circumstances of Jesus' life may not help us understand the relationship and God's love. It is the love that Jesus showed to others that offers us a glimpse of God's love. Jesus' love embraced all the people he met, those who accepted him and those who did not. Because of his intimate union with God, it was really divine love that Jesus offered to others. His was a universal, unselfish, merciful love, one that was offered to those who were easy to love and those who were not. Jesus' life revealed this love as the love he showed to others because it was the love he shared with God.

Jesus' self-emptying love points back to the self-emptying love of God and forward to the kind of self-emptying love expected of us. God's love was shown in the fact that the Son of God was sent into the world. This divine self-emptying, first by God and then by Jesus, is the kind of love to which we are all called. We are to love one another in the way Jesus loved us. It may seem strange to be commanded to love, for, as the lyrics of the song so rightly state, "I can't make you love me if you don't." Perhaps it is the radical nature of this love that requires a commandment.

Still, every one of us can point to examples of self-emptying love. When we really love another person, we are more than willing to relinquish our own comfort or desire for that person. Such love is alive and well in many families. Wives and husbands treat each other with understanding and tenderness; loving parents put the needs of their children above their own; adult children open their lives in order to care for their aging parents. Self-emptying love can also be found outside of our intimate circles. We find it in hospitals, in classrooms, and on battlefields. Unselfish people commit themselves to the service of those they love and, sometimes, those they do not even know. Such love is but a hint of the kind of love that God has for us.

This kind of love may not come easily at first. Today's reading from Acts demonstrates this. Initially Peter hesitated to move into the world of Cornelius, the Roman centurion. After all, Rome was the occupying force at the time and Roman soldiers had mocked and beaten Jesus and ultimately driven the nails into his body. Who could blame Peter if he hesitated? However, the story shows how the Spirit of God does not respect the religious, ethnic, or political divisions that may have held sway at the time. Even the Gentiles received the Spirit. Consequently, Peter realized that there was no excuse for withholding the blessings of baptism from those in the household of Cornelius.

In our lives there are genuine religious, ethnic, and political differences that separate, even alienate us from others. Even closer to home, we may be estranged from friends, neighbors, or members of our families. We cannot deny any of this. We are told, however, that we cannot rest in this estrangement or enmity. We are called to extend to others the kind of love that Jesus has for us. Is this really possible? How can we forgive? How can we move beyond the offenses perpetrated against us? Humanly speaking, there may be no answer to this. However, today's readings clearly insist that we must be open to all. Jesus calls us his friends and invites us to remain in his love. We are further told that we must love, because love is of God. Lest we wonder just what this means, we are given the example of Peter. This is the radical challenge facing us today. We cannot merely rest secure in our belief that "God is love." Easter calls us to live out this conviction in a world that is so burdened with conflict and strife. What's love got to do with it? Everything!

Praying with Scripture

- Where in your life do you find genuine self-emptying love?

- Pray for the grace to offer such love to others.

- Reach out this week to at least one person who is outside of your intimate circle of family and friends.

ASCENSION
Readings:
Acts 1:1–11; Ps 47:2–3, 6–9;
Eph 1:17–23 (or Eph 4:1–13);
Mark 16:15–20

JUST WHERE DID JESUS GO?

How high is up? How far up do you have to go before you fall down again? Is that where heaven is? If Jesus ascended into heaven, might we still find his body up there somewhere? Is it crowded up there? These are not merely inane questions that children might ask. And if the children do indeed ask them, what answers can we give? Actually, these are profound questions that touch on matters of cosmology, theology, and Christology. If religious seekers ask such questions, what answers do we give?

Few of us today still believe in a three-tiered world with earth in the middle, heaven above, and the netherworld beneath. Despite our rejection of such a conception of the world, many of us continue to frame our religious perceptions in line with this understanding. If prevailed upon, we might not claim that heaven is "up there," but we would be hard pressed to explain where it is. We might insist that it is a state of existence that transcends our present existence. With this, we probably do not mean the kind of parallel world of which the physicists speak. Strangely, we are no longer sure just what or where heaven is, but we certainly all want to go to heaven. So why not speak of heaven as "out there," as long as we do not limit "out there" to a spatial "out there"?

So how do we answer these questions? How high is up? It is beyond our comprehension, especially if we accept contemporary cosmology's claim that our universe is expanding at a rapid pace. How far up do you have to go before you fall down again? That depends upon the rate of the expansion. Is that where heaven is? It could be, as long as we do not limit heaven to spatial dimensions. If Jesus ascended into heaven, might we still find his body up there? Now *that* is the real question to ponder today.

The feast of the Ascension celebrates one aspect of the resurrection, namely, Jesus' exaltation. He did not wait for forty days to be glorified at God's right hand. That already happened at his resurrection. Limited human comprehension prevents us from even beginning to grasp the scope of this mystery. For this reason, throughout the Easter season we focus our attention first on one aspect of this mystery and then on another. On Easter day we concentrate on Jesus' victory over sin and death; today we reflect on his exaltation or enthronement. We will reflect on the gift of the Spirit at Pentecost.

The flow of the theology in today's readings carries us through the message to this feast. First, we stand with the disciples gazing up at the sky, not knowing what has happened or what it might mean for us. We were so happy that he had returned to us at the time of his resurrection. Like them, we might have expected a noticeable change in society as a result. (They looked for the reestablishment of the kingdom of Israel. What might we have expected?) And now he is gone again. Taken from our sight by a cloud. Now what are we to do?

It is in the second reading that Paul explains the theological meaning of Jesus' exaltation. He ascended to heaven to be enthroned in glory. This image recalls an ancient Near Eastern creation tradition. After cosmic chaos had been conquered by the creator-god and the celestial bodies had been assigned their heavenly places, a palace was erected for the triumphant deity and a throne set up from which that god ruled over heaven and earth. It was to this royal throne that Jesus ascended, there to sit at the creator-God's right hand.

Finally, it is in the gospel reading that we discover the commission given first to the disciples who witnessed Jesus' ascension and then to us: "Go into the whole world and proclaim the gospel." This certainly answers the question posed above: Now what do we do? We are to proclaim the gospel, and to do so to the whole world. This is a daunting task! However, we have been promised the power that comes with the Holy Spirit. Jesus may no longer be a tangible presence in our lives, but this does not mean that we are alone. Having conquered the chaos of sin and death, he is exalted with God, yet somehow he still lives with us.

The first reading states that with the ascension of Jesus, two men in white garments appeared next to the disciples and asked them: "Why are you standing there looking at the sky?" They might have added: You have work to do. You have a commission to fulfill. From now on, *you* are the body of Christ; *you* must proclaim the good news; *you* must drive out the demons that hold people in their addicting clutches; *you* must embrace all people with the merciful love of God. *You* now stand as an answer to the question: "Just where did Jesus go?"

Praying with Scripture

- How do you fulfill the commission to proclaim the gospel given by Jesus at the time of his ascension?

- Does your manner of living give witness to the triumph of Jesus, or does it suggest that chaos reigns supreme?

- Pray the responsorial psalm as a hymn of praise to our exalted Lord.

SEVENTH SUNDAY OF EASTER
Readings:
Acts 1:15–17, 20a, 20c–26;
Ps 103:1–2, 11–12, 19–20;
1 John 4:11–16; John 17:11b–19

IN-BETWEEN, BUT NOT ALONE!

How does one go on when life seems to have been torn apart at the seams? Loved ones die; others turn away from us; we are forced to assume responsibilities we never chose. Or we are forced to confront violence and hatred, disdain and alienation. We want things to be what they were before, but we know that they never will be. The world is just not the same, and we do not really like it the way it is.

Today's readings depict the disciples of Jesus in a liminal stage, a time "in-between," a time of change and transition. The Risen Christ had ascended to the right hand of God, but the Spirit had not yet descended upon them. Following the Easter story, we read that the group of Twelve is missing a member (Judas), and so Peter steps forward to lead the "early church" in one of its first administrative decisions, choosing a replacement for the one who had betrayed the Lord. The world was not the same for any of them. They were in a time "in-between," trying to cling to what they had known while realizing that things were no longer what they had been before. This "in-between" time was very frightening. It demanded that they rethink their priorities, reorder their lives, and reconstitute their community. They had been commissioned to further the teachings of Jesus and continue his ministry, and now they had to learn how to deal with this period of transition.

Liturgically, we too are in a liminal state, the time between the ascension of Jesus and the descent of the Holy Spirit. How are we to deal with the ambiguity of it? Today's readings offer us some direction. The first reading provides us a glimpse into the life of the early church. It shows a leader who involves the entire community in an important ecclesial decision, and a community that takes this ecclesial responsibility seriously. They first prayed together for guidance, and then together they chose Matthias as the twelfth apostle. As we today struggle with issues of church leadership and communal responsibility and we await the coming of the Spirit in all its fullness, we would do well to learn from this model of collegiality. Differences of opinion are understandable; strong commitment to one's point of view is inevitable. However, appreciation for the various roles played by members within the community, respect for the differing obligations that accompany those roles, openness to the insights that arise from diverse perspectives, and acknowledgment of the genuine love and commitment that reside in the heart of each member of the community are essential if the church is to be faithful to the Spirit that guides it.

The second reading for most of the Sundays of the Easter season comes from the First Letter of John. It directs our attention to love, the love that God has for us and, flowing from this love, the love we must have for one another. We are constantly reminded of the breadth and depth of this love and of its ability to transform us into new people. There is a lesson to be learned from this reading as well and, perhaps, it is the most important lesson of all. The love of God must be the driving force of our lives. It must be the reason we act as we do and choose as we choose. Jesus initiated us into this love so that we too might live in it and allow it to radiate from us. Jesus may have left us, but he bequeathed his love to us. And "whoever remains in love remains in God."

Today's gospel depicts a very tender moment in the life of Jesus. There we read that Jesus prays for us. He prays that we might be embraced by God's protective love as we continue life in this world. Jesus knew the challenges that we would have to face throughout life. He knew its disappointments. He certainly knew its hostility. We may not be happy with certain aspects of this world. We may feel disappointed and betrayed by religious and political leaders, by friends and family, by neighbors and companions in the workplace. However, this is the world that we have, and Jesus prayed that we might not be overcome by its difficulties.

Jesus may have departed this world, but not without having radically changed it. He taught us to love and to forgive; he taught us understanding and courage; he gave new meaning to life and told us to face death without despair. His teaching would be the foundation of a new world. We now live "in-between" the world we knew and loved and the one that is yet to appear, the one we are helping to fashion. We are "in-between," but we are not alone. We have a God who loves us, a redeemer who prays for us, and we also have each other.

Praying with Scripture

- Reflect on the many ways the love of God has been made known to you.

- What small acts of love can you perform that will make a difference in the life of just one person?

- Pray for those who, like you, need courage to go on.

PENTECOST
Readings:
Acts 2:1–11; Ps 104:1, 24, 29–31, 34;
1 Cor 12:3b–7, 12–13 (or Gal 5:16–25);
John 20:19–23 (or John 15:26–27; 16:12–15)

WHAT'S GOTTEN INTO YOU?

"What's gotten into you?" This question usually arises as a response to unacceptable behavior. But it is an appropriate question for today's feast. The very people who for days, even weeks, had hidden themselves in fear for their lives, were out and about and acting in astonishing ways. They no longer lived in secret. In fact, they were calling attention to themselves by their behavior. What had gotten into them?

"They were all filled with the Holy Spirit." Such a simple statement! So simple, so familiar that it may no longer startle us. These previously terrified people were now all somehow filled with the dynamic power of God; the power that refreshes and recreates, that comforts and heals; the power so eloquently acclaimed in today's sequence. This Spirit burned within them like tongues of fire, and they went forth and proclaimed the message of God's love manifested in the resurrection of Jesus. And a miracle took place. Though they spoke in their own tongue, their listeners understood the message in their respective languages. Clearly the Spirit of God was present, first emboldening the once frightened disciples and then opening the ears of the crowd to the marvels of the gospel message.

This same Spirit was given to us when we were baptized into the death and resurrection of Jesus and confirmed in the power of the Spirit. If we received the same Spirit, as did the disciples on that first Pentecost, why can't we do the same marvelous deeds? But we can! Paul assures us, as he did the Corinthians, that "to each individual the manifestation of the Spirit is given for some benefit." And to what benefit is the Spirit given? For the benefit of the community at large, not merely the individual possessing the special gift. In situations where hatred and violence prevail, believers bring kindness and gentleness; they are truly generous in a world in which greed and selfishness reign. Just as it did at the time of Pentecost, the Spirit of God transforms minds and hearts that are open to its healing power. Not everyone in the community will be able to perform the same service, but we have different gifts. We are one body in Christ, however, and together we will be able to accomplish much.

The Spirit that Jesus sent us from his Father is a Spirit of reconciliation. We may think that we cannot accomplish great feats, but God's Spirit will assist us in overcoming grudges and avoiding vengeance. This Spirit of truth will direct us into lives of honesty and integrity. Nations all over the world are hemorrhaging from the wounds of war; various religious groups live in constant fear of prejudice and persecution; church leadership has lost much credibility among the members and its moral voice has been muted within the broader society. We are certainly in desperate need of the transforming power of the Spirit. The words of today's Sequence, Come, O Holy Spirit, are more than timely:

> Heal our wounds, our strength renew;
> On our dryness pour your dew;
> Wash the stains of guilt away:
> Bend the stubborn heart and will;
> Melt the frozen, warm the chill;
> Guide the steps that go astray.

The first reading assures us of the universality of the transformation effected by the Spirit. Those who benefited from the transformation of the disciples were "devout Jews from every nation under heaven." The Diaspora or dispersion of the Jewish people resulting from the exile, once considered a searing sentence, can now be seen as a great boon to the missionary venture of the early church. With one sermon, people from every corner of the world have now heard the good news of the gospel. In another situation, some of these people could have been enemies. Now, they are sisters and brothers in faith, members of the same body of Christ. The distinctions Jew and Greek, slave and free, woman and man, rich and poor, educated and illiterate are no longer divisions; they are simply identifications of unique per-spectives of life. The Spirit of God seizes all who have opened themselves to the miracle of transformation.

This acceptance and cherishing of diversity are themselves a miracle of grace, a sign of the presence of the all-holy Spirit. They testify to us that old wounds have been healed and stubborn minds and wills have been softened. The desire to do what we can in our neighbors' and in our world, to work together with people of different backgrounds and faiths to change the world, to set aside our own preferences and biases are all fruits of the Spirit who has been given to us. The Holy Spirit, the dynamic power of God, has been bestowed on us in all fullness. And with that Spirit come the gifts and the courage we need to transform the world. The first disciples had their day, and they seized it with a gusto that has been remembered down through the centuries and is cel-ebrated in today's feast. This is our day. We now have a chance to show others what's gotten into us.

Praying with Scripture

- Spend a few moments prayerfully reading the Sequence for Pentecost: "Come, O Holy Spirit, come."

- What gift of the Spirit do you have to offer to the world?

- Support those who have other gifts to offer.

Ordinary Time

FIRST SUNDAY IN ORDINARY TIME: BAPTISM OF THE LORD

SECOND SUNDAY IN ORDINARY TIME

Readings:
1 Sam 3:3b–10, 19; Ps 40:2, 4, 7–10;
1 Cor 6:13c–15a, 17–20; John 1:35–42

Did You Call?

Nowadays we seem to be dissatisfied if we are considered ordinary. We seek to be the first or the best, or at least to belong to the group that is first or best. Yet, most of us are really quite ordinary people living ordinary lives. Despite this, there need be nothing ordinary about being ordinary. With this Sunday we enter the interlude between seasons. Christmas with its excitement and glitter is behind us and the sober experience of Lent followed by the glory of Easter is in the future. In the liturgical year, this is the period known as Ordinary Time. It is the time during which we reflect on the very ordinary ways that God enters our lives, thus making them extraordinary.

The first reading recounts an event in the early life of the prophet Samuel. As a young boy he lived in a religious shrine, entrusted to the keeping of the old priest Eli. One very ordinary evening he went to sleep and was awakened by a very strange occurrence. Both he and Eli, to whom he reported this occurrence, misunderstood what was happening. He thought that Eli was calling him; Eli thought that the boy was mistaken. Who could have imagined that God was calling Samuel out of sleep? Furthermore, who would have thought that God would choose a young boy, one with no power or prestige, someone whose chief responsibility was making sure that the light in the sanctuary was kept burning? Surely there were others more qualified.

A comparable situation is described in the gospel passage from John. In it Jesus appears to be so unremarkable that John the Baptist has to point him out to two of John's disciples. In this account, Jesus does nothing that will attract attention. He does not yet have a following. And, unlike his depiction in much religious art, he does not look or dress differently. He is just an ordinary Middle Eastern man. There is no miraculous healing that amazes the crowds; there is no dramatic instruction that mesmerizes his audience. He is simply passing by the people who are standing around. It is a very ordinary scene. Yet John knows who he is and informs his own disciples of Jesus' hidden identity: "Behold, the Lamb of God." It is only after the two men spend the day with Jesus that they realize how extraordinary he really is.

Perhaps what Paul describes in his Letter to the Corinthians is the most startling example of the extraordinary hidden within what is ordinary. He argues that ordinary human beings, by means of faith, are members of Christ. Their human bodies, thought weak and limited, are temples wherein dwells the Holy Spirit. He further claims that since God raised Jesus from the dead, God will also raise all those who are joined to Jesus. Paul insists here on the dignity of the ordinary human body, because he is condemning the licentious lives of many of the Corinthians. He is trying to show them that their immoral behavior is violating the very bodies purchased by Christ at the price of his blood.

In these three incidents, the extraordinary was not at first apparent. It takes eyes of faith to recognize it. Both Samuel and Eli initially misunderstood the voice, but when they realized that it was God calling in the night, they accepted its message. Paul rebuked the Corinthian Christians who had lost sight of their bodily dignity and were participating in illicit practices. Those who accepted his words glorified God though the morality of their lives. Initially the disciples of John saw nothing unusual in Jesus.

However, they listened to John's advice, spent the day with Jesus, and eventually became his disciples. At first, all of these people saw only what was obvious. In each instance, however, God called them to deeper insight through the agency of another.

We are not unlike these biblical people. We do not always look beneath the surface, and so we often miss the extraordinary in what is ordinary. We do not hear the voice of God in the voices of others calling us to great things, to sacrifice ourselves for our children, to give of ourselves to aging parents, to show concern to friends or neighbors. We do not recognize Christ in the thoughtful people with whom we work, the honest people with whom we do business, the understanding people who help us in simple ways, the ordinary people with whom we live.

It takes only a little effort to attune our ears to hear the voice of God, to adjust our sight to recognize Christ in our midst. As members of Christ, we have the Holy Spirit dwelling within us. This same Spirit urges us to reach out to others. What we accomplish may not be as impressive as what was accomplished by Samuel, or the first disciples of Jesus, or Paul. Results are up to God. All we have to be concerned about is that we recognize the call of God in the ordinary events of life and we respond: "Here I am. Did you call?"

Praying with Scripture

- Through whose voices might God be calling you?

- In what ways might the ordinary things you do actually be ministry?

- Do you respect your body as you should by living a moral and healthy life?

THIRD SUNDAY IN ORDINARY TIME

Readings:
Jonah 3:1–5, 10; Ps 25:4–9;
1 Cor 7:29–31; Mark 1:14–20

THE FISH STORY THAT TOPS ALL!

God seems to choose the most unlikely people to proclaim the good news. We find examples of this in today's readings. We first hear the story of a prophet who tried to escape his call and was carried to his ministry in the belly of a large fish. We then read from a letter written by a tentmaker who became a disciple of Jesus after the power of God knocked him down. Finally, we are told about simple fishermen who knew a lot about bait and nets, but very little about preaching. And God has not reversed this pattern today. The gospel is lived and taught by many faithful elementary school teachers who spend their days teaching reading, writing, and arithmetic, by stockbrokers who pay and sell shares all day long, by waiters who take orders and carry food, by doctors who listen to hearts and take pulses, clerks who file and retrieve forms, firefighters who risk their lives, and so on, all people who are probably so engrossed in their work that they may not give the gospel they are living quietly a second thought.

The message heard in both the first and the third readings is the same: Repent! Reform your lives! Believe in the gospel! And do it today! Stop taking advantage of each other! Forgive those who have offended you! Be patient with the quirks of others! Don't engage in gossip! Share what you have with those who are less fortunate! Be sensitive to the limits of the Earth's natural wealth! Believe in the gospel!

There is an urgency to this message. Paul tells us that "the time is running out"; Jesus declares that "the kingdom of God is at hand." Both are referring to the new age that is to come, the time of fulfillment. Their words imply that this age is about to dawn. The Greek language has two words for time: *chrónos,* which is normal linear time, and *kairós,* which is extraordinary time, "time out of time." Paul is talking about *kairós,* a critical time that calls for a very different manner of living, one that demonstrates that the new age of fulfillment has already arrived. Jesus proclaims that this new age, the *kairós*-time, is at hand, and like the prophets of old, he calls for a change of heart. Has it come? Or is it coming? Actually it is both; it has come and it is coming. It was inaugurated by Jesus but has not yet been brought to completion. It is continually brought to birth each time we transcend our selfish or sinful inclinations and live in a way that has been modeled for us by Jesus.

The challenge placed before us today is sobering. Jonah was directed by God to deliver the message of salvation to the Ninevites, a nation considered an enemy of the ancient Israelites. They were a people known for their brutality. It is no wonder that Jonah fled in the opposite direction. When he finally did preach to the Ninevites, however, the entire nation repented. Paul exhorts us today to live in this world as if we were not living in it. What does this mean? Just what does this new age demand? What is God expecting of us? Certainly Paul is not condemning human life or the world in which we live it. Rather, he is saying that there is more to life than weeping or rejoicing or buying or using. We are not to live merely in order to derive pleasure and satisfaction for ourselves. Rather, we are to be concerned with the well-being of a nation that has proven itself our enemy. We are to live in opposition to the pleasure-seeking standards of society. Who can do this? Who even wants to do it?

The fish theme found in the first reading appears again in the gospel. The difference is, of course, that Jonah did not catch a fish; he was caught by one. The four disciples were already fishermen, but were told that there were bigger fish to catch. If they followed Jesus, they too would have a good fish story to tell. So "they abandoned their nets and followed him." And they were successful. They found people ready and willing to be transformed. There are such people today as well. We have all heard of soldiers who place themselves in harm's way in order to protect civilians caught in the terrors of war. We have watched emergency personnel disregard their own safety and rush into dangerous situations for the sake of others. We know parents and grandparents who deny themselves pleasure and comfort in favor of their children and grandchildren. Heroic actions often stem from doing what simply has to be done despite any difficulty, and we all know people who act in this way.

If we act out of compassion rather than from indifference, out of understanding rather than disdain, out of kindness rather than selfishness, we will indeed bring about the fullness of the kingdom of God. And we will have a story to tell that will top even Jonah's.

Praying with Scripture

- Where in your life might God be calling you to repent and reform?

- What are you already doing that indicates you are living in the new age?

- In what ways might God be calling you to minister to others?

FOURTH SUNDAY IN ORDINARY TIME

Readings:
Deut 18:15–20; Ps 95:1–2, 6–9;
1 Cor 7:32–35; Mark 1:21–28

WHERE HAVE ALL THE RESOLUTIONS GONE?

We are far enough into the New Year to ask: "Where have all the resolutions gone?" Every year we begin with good intentions and a certain amount of fervor, but it does not take long before we must admit that something has gone wrong. Either we tried to do more than we could in too short a time, or we became discouraged when long-standing bad habits did not melt away like snow during an early thaw, or we simply lost interest and sank back into the routine of life. Whatever the case may be, our resolutions have been shelved until next New Year, when once again we will be filled with enthusiasm and goodwill. It is unfortunate if we feel this way, for the readings of Ordinary Time continually remind us of the responsibilities that are ours as disciples of Jesus, and these responsibilities require that we resolve to improve our lives. However, the readings for the Sundays in Ordinary Time do not require that we change all at once. They offer such insights into this transformation one at a time.

Why would we be willing to accept the demands of discipleship and change our way of living? Because we know that we have habits that we should break and that we cherish attitudes that we should change. In some ways we might even have made a convenient truce with the forces of evil that roam freely in the world today, forces such as complacency in the face of poverty and injustice, religious or racial bias, an unwillingness to forgive. We know that we should change. That is why we make New Year's resolutions. However, discipleship calls for more than a promise to eat less or exercise regularly. It calls for a real, even though gradual, transformation of mind and heart.

Today's gospel tells the story of an exorcism. A man was possessed by an unclean spirit. The people at the time of Jesus believed that the world was the battlefield of a deadly conflict between the forces of good and evil. In line with this, all the suffering in the world was caused by demons that took control of people's lives. This explains why the gospels recount so many situations where Jesus casts out a demon. Each exorcism was a victory of good over evil, a defeat of the power of demons and the establishment of the reign of God. Often this evil took the form of some physical malady. Such was the case with the man in today's gospel, though his physical ailment is not identified. The demon appears to be unwilling to relinquish control of the man, for his departure is marked by the man's convulsions. This may appear to be an insignificant victory, but this is how the battle against the forces of evil is won; this is how the reign of God is established—little by little.

We no longer entertain the world view held by our religious ancestors, but we cannot deny that we are often caught in a battle between the forces of good and evil. Sometimes we even use the same language and speak about "our demons." We may be using the language metaphorically, but we cannot deny that at times we find ourselves under the control of habits that are detrimental to our well-being. Like the man in the gospel, we might need something as drastic as an exorcism to release us from their grip. And if we do not have the inner strength to keep simple New Year's resolutions, how can we hope to overcome these demons?

We do not all have to enroll in a rehab program, but we do need help if we are to change our lives. And God promised to send this help. The first reading reports this promise. Moses announced: "A prophet like me will the LORD, your God, raise up for you from among your own kin." This prophet would be chosen by God from within the people themselves and would speak God's own words with God's authority. From this passage grew the tradition that the Messiah would be a prophet. The gospel identifies Jesus as one who taught with such authority. His words and actions show that he has conquered the forces of evil. However, this victory must be realized in the life of each one of us. The reign of God must be established little by little.

There have always been many and varied voices that claim to have the remedy for our ills. Preachers have stirred up crowds and ignited emotions. Promises of healing have been made, yet the inner conflict that we suffer goes on and the demons continue to hold us by the throat. But then a voice is heard in the midst of the chaos of our lives, in the rubble of our broken resolutions. This voice rings with authority: Be quiet! Come out.

Praying with Scripture

- What are the "demons" with which you struggle?

- Pray for the courage to open yourself to the saving power of God's love.

- Make a new and worthwhile New Year's resolution.

FIFTH SUNDAY IN ORDINARY TIME

Readings:
Job 7:1–4, 6–7; Ps 147:1–6;
1 Cor 9:16–19, 22–23; Mark 1:29–39

THE LONG AND THE SHORT OF IT

Job seems so pessimistic: Life is a drudgery; "I have been assigned months of misery"; I am filled with restlessness! Will this ever end? And in the next breath he declares: "My days are swifter than a weaver's shuttle"; "My life is like the wind"; where did the time go?

And that is the long and short of it. At times, life is an unbearable burden thrust upon us. The days drag, and we drag ourselves through them. And then, again, time seems to slip through our fingers. We close our eyes for a moment and years rush by. Are we merely victims of fate? Pawns on some vast cosmic chessboard? Brought into the game of life by a decision not our own and dealt a hand over which we have no control? Is there really a God out there who cares what happens to each and every one of us?

Who has not entertained such questions when life turns an uncaring, or even terrifying face toward us? At such times it takes both faith and courage to believe that God does indeed heal the brokenhearted. But the gospel shows Jesus doing just that. He brought healing with a gentle touch and with words of power.

Jesus could sympathize with our burdens because they were his as well. He watched those whom he knew and loved diminish physically before his very eyes. He lived at a time when his country was occupied by a foreign force. He knew the consequences of armed conflict. It was for the purpose of lessening human burdens that he went about preaching and driving out demons. We might be tempted to wonder why, if he was so powerful, he allowed suffering to take hold in the first place. Why were people afflicted with disease or possessed by demons? And today we wonder: Why do the elderly poor languish in the cold? Why do innocent children bloat from malnutrition? Why is our future cut down on the battlefield? Why have we been assigned months of misery?

Questions like these have never really been satisfactorily answered. Instead of telling us *why*, Jesus shows us *how*. Without denying our own need for comfort, he directs our gaze toward the needs of others. How are we to deal with the tragedies of life? We are to approach those who suffer, grasp their hands, help them up; we are to heal the brokenhearted and bind up their wounds.

Paul learned this lesson well. Following the example of Jesus, he offered himself in service of others, becoming all things to all people. Can we do less? Can we continue to allow the elderly to languish? Or the children to starve? Or hatred to rule the world? Can we continue to allow misunderstanding to fester in our families, alienating us from those with whom we share life? Can we continue to support bigotry or indifference? Can we continue to allow such demons to possess us today?

At the time of Jesus, people believed that the world was the scene of a mortal battle between good and evil forces that were cosmic in nature, but that played out their conflict in human history. These forces were represented by angels and demons. Understanding this perspective, we realize that the gospel story is not only an account of healing and exorcism, but also one that describes the power of God in Jesus casting out the forces of evil in the world and establishing there the reign of God.

Today our understanding of the structure of the cosmos may reflect more closely to that of Albert Einstein than of the gospel writer. However, the ancient perspective does provide a way of understanding some of the suffering in life. We are indeed at war, not only with some identified human opponent, but also with forces of evil that are much more widespread in scope. And the battle is fought within each one of us.

It is not only addictive personalities that seem to be possessed. In a sense, we all have our demons. Traditionally, we have referred to these mysterious destructive forces as the seven capital sins: pride, anger, envy, jealousy, lust, avarice, and sloth. They may come disguised in different garb today, but these are the demons with which we all struggle. Every evil in the world can be traced back to one or more of these forces.

Job is right to cry out against such a life. So are we, for if we merely accept it, we will do nothing to change it. If we do not acknowledge the demons that seem to hold sway in our lives, in our world, we will not struggle to cast them out. Although the readings for today begin with a cry of desperation, they end on a note of triumph. The suffering people in the gospel came to Jesus and were healed and set free. If, like them, we seek him out and open ourselves to the power of his compassion, the forces of evil in our lives and in our world can be driven out and the reign of God will be established. This burdensome life really does hold promise.

Praying with Scripture

- Reflect on the suffering in the world and try to trace it back to one of the seven capital sins.

- Which of these demons has control in your life? What might you have to do to cast it out?

- How might the compassion of Jesus work through you to heal the brokenhearted?

SIXTH SUNDAY IN ORDINARY TIME
Readings:
Lev 13:1–2, 44–46; Ps 32:1–2, 5, 11;
1 Cor 10:31—11:1; Mark 1:40–45

NOT IN MY NEIGHBORHOOD!

Sometimes we may be willing to support good works as long as they are not set up in our neighborhood. It may be true that property value plummets when someone opens a halfway house or a hospice around the corner. This decline in value may also happen when the owners of that trendy ethnic restaurant move into the house next door. It is possible for us to agree that people have a right to live and prosper and receive the care that they need. But does this have to happen in our neighborhood?

There are valid reasons for forcing some people to make their "abode outside the camp." The first and third readings for this Sunday provide us with an example of this. Though the readings are really concerned with the reincorporation of the outcast into the community, it might be helpful to understand something of the reason for the forced separation.

Leprosy, or whatever the skin disease might have been, was considered contagious. Thus, the one afflicted with the disease was relegated to total isolation. Because the well-being of the entire community was at stake, quarantine was practiced as a precaution. In a community-based society such as ancient Israel, such separation from the community was virtually a death sentence. Thus, at the very time of greatest vulnerability the one suffering from the loathsome disease was deprived of community support. On the other hand, the possibility of contagion made the community understandably reluctant to allow the one afflicted to participate in community life. This type of disease did indeed create a complicated situation, but it did not always result in permanent alienation. Both readings show that the separation might be only temporary. When the danger was eliminated, the individual could be brought back into the community.

"Outcast" may sound strong, but there are still unspoken attitudes that keep some people "outside of the camp," and this often happens when they are in greatest need of community support. Many of us still shun those whose bodies are ravaged by an illness even though it is not contagious; we frequently avoid the company of friends or acquaintances who are consumed by grief at the death of a loved one; we keep our distance from people who speak with an unfamiliar accent; and we are suspicious of others whose religious beliefs and practices do not conform to ours. It is one thing to keep dangerous people "outside the camp," since they do, after all, threaten the security of the community. But are these people really dangerous? They may annoy us or make us feel uneasy; their presence may unsettle the comfort of our structured lives, but how do they threaten our safety?

There is probably not a person alive who has not at some time felt like an outcast, and all because some people will have nothing to do with certain races or ethnic groups, with people of a particular age or gender, social or economic standing or level of education, with individuals who have a different sexual preference. Reasons for keeping us "outside the camp" may have had no grounding other than the fact that we did not belong to the neighborhood. We know how such rejection feels, and yet we do the same to others.

How would Jesus respond? The answer is quite clear; we see it in the gospel. He would be moved with pity. He would stretch out his healing hand to the outcast and say: "Be made clean." Come join the community. And what would he say to those who tend to exclude others? They too need healing, and so he would be moved with pity toward them as well. He would stretch out that same hand and say: Avoid giving offense, whether to the Jews or Greeks, or to those burdened with illness or mourning the dead, or to the newly migrated or religiously different.

This should not surprise us for, after all, Jesus too experienced being an outcast. And why was he forced "outside the camp"? Because he was different. Though he did belong to the community, he didn't think like the rest of the group. He welcomed the outcast; he embraced the very people that others shunned. No one was beyond the circle of his compassion. No one was kept out of his neighborhood. And for this he was ostracized and ultimately silenced.

The silencing of Jesus' compassion was not final, however. Paul, who proclaimed the gospel to Jew and Greek alike, is evidence of the ongoing power of this compassion. He exhorted his hearers: "Be imitators of me, as I am of Christ." Down through the ages there have been others who continued this openness: Francis of Assisi kissed a man with leprosy; at the risk of their own lives, women and men welcomed runaway slaves into their homes; after September 11, 2001, Catholic high school girls wore head scarves in support of their Muslim friends. The embrace of Christ is without bounds; the neighborhood is expanding.

Praying with Scripture

- Remember your own experience of feeling like an outcast. Thank God for drawing you back into the circle of belonging and care.

- Pray for the insight to understand why you hold some people at a distance.

- Ask God for the courage to open your heart to them.

SEVENTH SUNDAY IN ORDINARY TIME
Readings:
Isa 43:18–19, 21–22, 24b–25;
Ps 41:2–5, 13–14;
2 Cor 1:18–22; Mark 2:1–12

NO PROBLEM!

We have many expressions for assuring each other that the mistakes we have made will not be held against us. The most familiar include: "I forgive you"; "don't worry about it"; "that's OK"; and more recently—"no problem." These are simple expressions, but they have the power to ease anxiety or repair broken relationships. They encourage us to look hopefully to the future rather than remain bogged down in the past.

We do not have to live long to realize how desperately we need to be forgiven. Little children often plead: "Don't be mad at me!" Mutual understanding and forbearance are at the heart of open and meaningful love relationships. Social harmony requires that we not take offense each time we feel misunderstood or overlooked. Finally, if there is ever to be peace in the world, nations have to get beyond the enmity and mistrust that they may have been harboring for years, even centuries, resulting in their fierce refusal to forgive each other.

Forgiveness does not mean that we close our eyes to the wrongs committed. Children are indeed frequently mischievous; friends and lovers sometimes do betray our trust; neighbors or social companions can certainly treat us poorly; and nations often do violate the rights of other nations. Nor are these always innocent mistakes. But forgiveness can work miracles. When we experience it from another, burdens are lifted from our shoulders, and life seems to hold new possibilities. We are assured that we are acceptable even though we are weak and make mistakes. Forgiveness is a precious gift that must never be taken for granted. Then, in turn, when we are in a position to forgive, forgiveness should not be withheld. Instead, it should be given generously, just as God grants it to us.

Today's readings move us step-by-step from the acknowledgment of wrongdoing, through forgiveness received, to the promise of new possibilities. With the psalmist we cry out: "O Lord, have pity on me; / heal me, though I have sinned against you." We often find it very difficult to admit that we have done something wrong, or even that we have made a simple mistake. Such admission seems an affront to our dignity, suggesting that we are less than we think we are, or that we would like others to think we are. Deep in our hearts, however, we know that if we are to be honest, we must admit our guilt.

The gospel offers a striking portrayal of the eagerness of Jesus to forgive. There we see the paralytic man being lowered into the room through the roof. He believed that Jesus could heal him of his physical ailment, and because of his faith he received even more than he had hoped. He walked out of the house a new man. Faith in the power of Jesus worked a miracle. Actually, it worked two miracles: the forgiveness of sin and the healing of infirmity.

In the first reading, Isaiah speaks of the newness, the second chance that is given to us by our gracious God: "Remember not the events of the past … ; / see, I am doing something new!" The image that the prophet uses sounds a chord of hope. God provides a way for us through the deserts of our lives; rivers of life-giving water appear in the wastelands of human experience. Though our sinfulness may have swept away our sense of peace and well-being, God promises: "Your sins I remember no more."

It is most consoling to realize that we have been forgiven, first by God and then by others. However, we experience something quite different when we are called on to forgive others. The challenge placed before us at such times is often measured by the hurt or anger that we have to bear. It is much easier to overlook the failings of little children than it is to forgive adults who should know better. The more serious the offense suffered, the harder it is to be open to the offender.

Is it too much to hope for genuine forgiveness coupled with the willingness to change one's life? Some would say "yes," and they might consider attempts at reconciliation signs of foolhardiness. Others are more hopeful, and they would regard these attempts as signs of great generosity of heart. There are husbands and wives who do forgive each other and recommit themselves to mutual respect and love. Not everyone operates according to the principle: "One strike and you're out!" Perhaps one of the most remarkable examples is the movement toward reconciliation taking place today in South Africa.

Finally, Jesus did not heal the paralytic man on condition that he embark on a new way of living. God seems to forgive us *first*. It is the realization of having been forgiven that then prompts us to change our lives for the better. Hence, the words we use in forgiving may seem trite, but our acts of forgiveness are often marvelously transformative.

Praying with Scripture

- Reflect upon and be grateful for the healing that you experienced as the result of having been forgiven.

- Pray for the generosity of heart to forgive someone who has offended you.

- Be courageous! Take steps toward reconciliation with someone from whom you may be estranged.

EIGHTH SUNDAY IN ORDINARY TIME

Readings:
Hos 2:16b, 17b, 21–22;
Ps 103:1–4, 8, 10, 12–13;
2 Cor 3:1b–6; Mark 2:18–22

New Life in Christ

Last Sunday we reflected on the new life that forgiveness from God and from others can offer us. We saw that if we are the ones forgiven, we must change our way of living so that we no longer offend others; if we are the ones forgiving, we must refrain from bringing up time and again the offense that caused us to suffer. Today we look at this startling newness from a different point of view. We consider what we must leave behind as we move into this new way of living. The new life challenges us to rid ourselves of any selfish, cynical, or destructive attitudes to which we have grown accustomed.

The words of Hosea found in the first reading are both tender and demanding. The spousal imagery depicts a passionate God wooing Israel. This courtship occurred in the desert, a place of deprivation. There are two reasons for this choice of venue. First, the desert was the place where God first made a covenant with the people. Thus a return to the desert indicated leaving behind the life of unfaithfulness that the people were living and returning to the innocence of first love. The desert was also chosen as a place of recommitment because of its barrenness. The prosperity that the people enjoyed had turned many of them away from God. God did not want anything to compete for Israel's attention, for God required total commitment. The relationship forged anew in the desert was meant to be grounded in righteousness and justice, in love and mercy, and it was destined to last forever. Who could possibly turn down such an offer? Still, it required a change of attitude and behavior—and this has always been difficult.

95

The gospel reading employs various metaphors to distinguish even more dramatically between the newness to which we are called and the old life that we must leave behind. First, Jesus chooses the image of a wedding to characterize the transition from one form of life into another. Various levels of transformation are suggested by means of this metaphor. Next he compares old cloth with new. The first type has already lost its shape and quality. It cannot bear too much tension, for it will easily pull apart. The second type is both sturdy and flexible, able to endure normal stress without danger of unraveling. The metaphor of wineskins is similar to that of cloth. Disintegrating wineskins cannot hold robust wine. Its expansion from ongoing fermentation will cause the wineskins to stretch, perhaps beyond their capacity. If this happens, the skins will be destroyed and the rich wine lost. In like manner, the new life of God's forgiveness and love cannot be contained within the negative patterns of the old life. It is just too vibrant, too brimming with possibilities.

The Christians of Corinth underwent this transformation of life. That ancient city enjoyed all the blessings a seaport might promise. Ships from all over the world brought interesting people and exotic treasures. As a result of this remarkable traffic, the city entertained customs and practices from various cultures of the world. Its trade made it prosperous. However, its cosmopolitan character was not an unmixed blessing. The itinerant nature of many people provided them with a freedom that resulted in various forms of depravity. Prosperity resulted in excess; autonomy often led to recklessness. Ancient Corinth was notorious for its licentiousness. Paul's task in converting the Corinthians and calling them away from such a life-style must have been daunting. However, he himself recognized the success of his ministry. Rather than seek letters of recommendation from them, needed by him as he traveled to a new site of missionary endeavor, he considered the Corinthians themselves his "letter of recommendation." They had obviously turned their lives around and were now living a new life in Christ through the power of the Spirit of God.

In many ways, contemporary society resembles both that of Israel at the time of Hosea and that of ancient Corinth. Many of us certainly benefit from advantages similar to those enjoyed by these societies. Likewise, we are guilty of many of their excesses.

However, God did not abandon them to their negligent lives. Rather, God invited them into a new way of living, one that flowed from and was nourished by a new commitment to God. By means of our own baptism, each of us is born into a new life. For Christians, this new life is the life of Christ lived in the Spirit. With it come new responsibilities. We too are called to leave behind our old ways of selfishness and greed, of anger and vindictiveness, of personal gratification and indifference toward others. We are called to live in righteousness and justice, in love and mercy, to use the words of the prophet Hosea. It is up to us to decide how we will respond to this call. Will we embrace the opportunity of a new life? Will someone ever be able to boast of our fidelity to the gospel, as Paul did of the Corinthians?

Praying with Scripture

- Prayerfully renew your baptismal promises. What in your life must you change in order to live the new life in Christ?

- Choose one or two works of justice, mercy, or love that will characterize your new life.

- Reflect on ways that you witness to a new life in Christ.

NINTH SUNDAY IN ORDINARY TIME
Readings:
Deut 5:12–15; Ps 81:3–8, 10–11;
2 Cor 4:6–11; Mark 2:23—3:6

AT LAST IT'S SUNDAY!

Why is Sunday considered a special day? Children, of course, are happy with it because there is no school on Sunday. For many adults, it is a day away from work. That is, unless one brings work home and turns the day into a time to "catch up." Some people argue that the best television news commentators appear on programs that are aired on Sunday morning. Then, in the afternoon, one can watch "the game." It is obvious from today's first reading and gospel passage that the biblical authors had something entirely different in mind when they emphasized the importance of the Sabbath.

Sabbath and Sunday are not the same. Sabbath, from the Hebrew word for *rest,* is the seventh day of the week, while Sunday, the first day of the week, is regularly observed by Christians. Sabbath is found with two biblical traditions. The first and probably more familiar account is found in Exodus, where it links the Sabbath with God's "rest" at the completion of creation. As God rested on the seventh day, so should Israel (Exod 21:11; Gen 2:2–3). Today's reading is from Deuteronomy. Here the emphasis is not on the reason for Sabbath observance itself, but on the rest from labor granted to slaves as well. This regulation is grounded in the theme of deliverance. As God showed favor to the Israelites when they were slaves, so should the Israelites show favor to other slaves. (The point here is not slavery, which was not abolished, but observance of the Sabbath, which was rigorously enforced.)

Why was it so important to refrain from work on the Sabbath? It was probably not the work itself, but the fact of setting of the day apart as a special day, when normal activity ceased and attention was turned to God and the things of God. Rest from the kind of labor required for survival became a way of acknowledging total dependence on God. Showing leniency to slaves was a further reminder of absolute reliance on God. It was the attitudes expressed more than the practices themselves that demonstrated the people's religious devotion.

One of the most bitterly contested issues Jesus faced during his ministry was his apparent disregard for Sabbath observance. Today's gospel reading illustrates this. The Pharisees accused the disciples of "reaping," clearly a violation of Sabbath law. Referring to a story about David, Jesus reminds them that genuine human need supersedes even some religious laws. In a second episode, the Pharisees censure Jesus for healing on the Sabbath. Once again he insists that doing good is more important than rigid adherence to religious practice. Jesus does not disregard the Sabbath. Instead, he places concern for the distress of others above even authentic observance.

The first Christians continued to observe the Sabbath (Acts 13:14), but they also gathered on the first day of the week to "break bread" (Acts 20:7). Thus Sunday became the day to celebrate the Eucharist. When they were finally separated from the synagogue, they observed Sunday alone as the Lord's Day. While Sunday was certainly the first day of the calendar week, it was also considered the eighth day, the day inaugurating the "new age" of fulfillment.

Several significant lessons can be learned from today's readings. First, they highlight the importance of setting aside time as "sacred time," time that we commit to that mysterious power that brought us into this world and continues to sustain us in its love. It is so easy to be swept away in the rush of everyday living, with all of its demands and the enjoyment that it offers. We need regular time to step back and reflect on how we have been blessed by a gracious God. "The Lord's Day" is just such a time.

Second, we need time to remember that, as weighty as our work might be, we are not the motivating force that holds everything together or moves everything to its completion. The world, and even our work, can be carried on without us. It is so easy to forget this when we are consumed with our own importance. We need to step back at times and take our hands off the wheel, or the computer, or whatever it is that we operate, and realize that the whole world is in God's hands and not in ours. "The Lord's Day" is a time for such reflection.

Third, devotional practices are meant to set the Sabbath apart from all other days as holy, and to provide opportunities to express our religious sentiments. These practices are meant to be vehicles of grace. When they are regarded as simply regulations to follow, however, they can become irrelevant and burdensome, as they seem to be pictured in the gospel account. "The Lord's Day" is meant to be a day of genuine religious celebration.

It is up to us to make sure that the special character of Sunday is not lost. It is not simply another day in a routine week. Rather, it is sacred time set aside for God and the things of God.

Praying with Scripture

- In what ways do you set Sunday apart from the rest of the week?

- How might you make Sunday religious practices more meaningful?

- How can you lessen the burden that others are made to bear on Sunday?

TENTH SUNDAY IN ORDINARY TIME
Readings:
Gen 3:9–15; Ps 130:1–8;
2 Cor 4:13—5:1; Mark 3:20–35

THE DEVIL MADE ME DO IT!

It is not only children who hide behind excuses like this. It has always been difficult for us to take responsibility for our mistakes. We might not blame "the devil," but there are many other convenient scapegoats such as a deprived childhood or overindulgent parents; some form of physical, mental, or emotional deficiency, or a permissive society, to name but a few. Each one of these sets of circumstances may well prevent an individual from developing into the best person possible, but it would be an error to place the blame for evil in the world on any one of them.

Just what is the origin of evil in the world? The readings for today attempt to answer that question. The passage from the Book of Genesis carefully sketches the story of the first sin as it occurred in the garden. It is also a story of passing the blame; the man blames the woman, and then she blames the serpent. The story is a reinterpretation of an ancient myth explaining humankind's entrance into the civilized world, the allurements there that will tempt women and men alike, and the consequences that they have to endure for their wrong decisions. In Israel's version of the story, God does not engage in this "blame game." The man, the woman, and the serpent all had a hand in the transgression, and so all of them are made to pay the penalty. Furthermore, contrary to a popular misconception, the serpent is not the devil. In fact, the serpent is called "the most cunning of all the animals the Lord God made" (Gen 3:1). Though "cunning" is usually understood here in a negative fashion, it also carries the positive meaning of "skillful" or "prudent." The serpent clearly posed a temptation, just as money, reputation, or physical beauty tempts us today. However, the serpent was not "the devil."

The gospel certainly refers to demons and Satan. Some of the scribes argued that Jesus was able to exercise power over demons because he himself was possessed by the prince of demons. This challenge reflects the ancient view of the world as the battlefield on which was waged the conflict between the forces of good and evil. Jesus refutes the accusation by insisting that armed forces do not fight against themselves; Satan against Satan would not be able to stand. On the contrary, Jesus drives out demons through the power of God. Though Jesus counters their false claim, he does not challenge the world view that includes demons. So, is the devil the cause of the evil in the world? Is there really a battle in the world between the forces of good and evil?

The second question is easier to answer than the first. No one will deny that there is evil in the world, and that that evil is at war with what is good. We know from experience that we are in a constant struggle between good and evil. We see it in the world at large. Good people war with one another; unjust economic systems that were set up to help people exploit the vulnerable. Groups committed to various goals demean those who disagree with them. In our families we may encounter infidelity, abuse, and alienation. We find in ourselves strains of addiction, resentments, and despair. We who are the offspring of the woman in the garden are in constant enmity with the offspring of the serpent.

On the other hand, there is quite a bit of theological debate over the origin of evil. Since our view of the world is very different from that of the ancient Israelites and early Christians, many people no longer believe in demons that are responsible for evil. They further argue that the idea of forces of evil in the world at odds in the world with the forces of good moves us very close to the concept of dualism, a concept that does not correspond well with strict monotheism. This does not mean that they reject the idea of evil itself. On the contrary, they place the blame squarely on the shoulders of sinful human beings.

While there is often a close connection between evil and suffering, the cause of suffering is quite a different matter. We are limited creatures who are subject to the laws of nature. This fact has enabled various branches of science to discover the causes of much of the suffering we must endure. But science has not uncovered the source of moral evil. If demons are not responsible for moral evil, who is? Is God? The immediate answer to that question is: "No! God is all good!" If not God or demons, then who? The only ones left to blame are human beings, and we all know that this is not an unfair accusation. We may not be the cause of all our suffering, but we, as the worldwide community, are responsible for the moral evil in the world. God created us with the capacity for freedom and self-determination, and at times we choose what is wrong. Acknowledging this, we can no longer hide behind the excuse: "The devil made me do it!"

Praying with Scripture

- What acts for you as a temptation to sin? How do you deal with it?

- In what ways do you contribute to the moral evil present in the world?

- Pray for the courage to take responsibility for your sinfulness.

ELEVENTH SUNDAY IN ORDINARY TIME

Readings:
Ezek 17:22–24; Ps 92:2–3, 13–16;
2 Cor 5:6–10; Mark 4:26–34

LIKE A MUSTARD SEED

I once saw a simple pendant the size of a small marble. It was clear plastic and in the middle was a tiny mustard seed. I was, of course, reminded of the parable found in today's gospel, and I wondered at the possibilities that this tiny speck might hold. But when you think about it, everything comes from some kind of tiny seed; even each one of us did. Cosmologists tell us that the universe itself developed from the tiniest subatomic particle. The marvel of it boggles the mind. Just imagine—all of that potential packed into something that is too small to be detected even with our most powerful instruments. This is precisely what today's readings would have us consider. With great poetic insight, both the reading from the prophet Ezekiel and the passage from the gospel draw on the seed metaphor to demonstrate the astonishing miracle of natural growth and the equally astonishing mystery of hidden potential.

The majestic cedar described in Ezekiel's fable began as a tender shoot cut from the topmost branch of another tree. It took years to grow into the magnificent tree that it finally became. As is the case with all living beings, the growth was incremental, so gradual that in all probability its progress went undetected. The lofty mountain upon which it was planted may well have been the most challenging place for new seedlings. With little or no protection against inclement weather, its growth could have been compromised and its very survival placed in jeopardy. However, this was a shoot from a cedar, the hardy tree that thrives on mountaintops. Most likely the tender shoot was actually strengthened by the weather of the high altitude. Then, when it had grown, it added majesty to the mountain, and it served as home for all of the birds that ventured to the heights.

The prophet adds another very interesting theme, that of reversal:

> ...bring low the high tree,
>   lift high the lowly tree,
> wither up the green tree,
>   and make the withered tree bloom.

This cedar seems to be replacing other trees, trees that may have taken upon themselves a status and sense of entitlement that were not intrinsically theirs. These trees are now displaced and humbled, while the imposing cedar rises to prominence and is sought out by the birds as a safe haven. Ezekiel was talking about the restoration of the nation of Israel. Though it had been humiliated in defeat and exile, God would build it up again. This in itself is an encouraging message.

The parables that we read in the gospel have a similar meaning. The seed that is scattered in the field and the mustard seed that is sown in the ground are very insignificant. However, they carry great potential within themselves. Their growth is not an overnight phenomenon, but when they do reach their full potential, overcoming all obstacles, the first yields a bountiful harvest and the second becomes the abode of the birds of the sky. Jesus employs these parables to describe the reign of God, the new way of living that he came to proclaim. This way of living begins in very ordinary circumstances with apparently insignificant acts. But these acts are pregnant with extraordinary potential, and this potential gradually matures until it has spread itself far and wide.

Just as plant growth is imperceptible, so the development of the reign of God often escapes our awareness. In fact, as Paul tells us today, while we are living in this life, "we walk by faith, not by sight." We should not misunderstand. There is a definite difference between plant growth and the development of the reign of God. We may have to wait a long time, but eventually we will be able to see the plant's progress. On the other hand, time alone will not reveal the action of God in the world today. We need eyes of faith for that. But then if we have eyes of faith, we will recognize the reign of God struggling to be realized in our midst everywhere and at all times, and we will not have to wait for a culminating event.

Where will we find the reign of God? Where should we look? We will find it unfolding in our homes whenever we are patient with or forgiving toward those with whom we live. We will recognize it in the helping hand extended to us at school or at work, in the gentle and healing touch of health caretakers, in the strong arms of those on whom we depend. We will appreciate it in the honesty with which financial or business transactions are conducted, in the willingness of others to provide for us in our need, in the courage of women and men who place themselves in harm's way for the sake of others. The reign of God is like an insignificant seed, overlooked by most, but cherished by those who know that it is brimming with potential.

Praying with Scripture

- Ask God for the grace to recognize the reign of God in the goodness of others.

- Foster the growth of the reign of God by performing one or two genuine acts of kindness this week.

- Pray the Lord's Prayer slowly and thoughtfully, reflecting particularly on the phrase "thy kingdom come."

TWELFTH SUNDAY IN ORDINARY TIME
Readings:
Job 38:1, 8–11; Ps 107:23–26, 28–31;
2 Cor 5:14–17; Mark 4:35–41

WHAT IS GOD LIKE?

One of the hotly debated topics consistently found on the front burner of discussion is the relationship between God and science. Ever since the Enlightenment, when the Western world came to appreciate many of the physical laws that govern the world in which we live, we have wondered how these new insights might affect the way we understand God. Some people contend that scientific knowledge has replaced faith in God. For them, the laws of nature now explain much of the mystery of the world. Others insist that while science and religion are not at odds with each other, neither are they companions in the same search for meaning. Science is interested in the "how" of things, while religion is concerned with "why." Still others argue that there must be some compatibility between science and religion, because they are both committed to the discovery of truth, and truth cannot be divided against itself.

Today's readings remind us of how the relationship between God and the natural world was perceived by our religious ancestors. These people may not have possessed the kind of scientific knowledge that we do today, but neither were they ignorant of the powers of nature. The ancestors of Israel came from Mesopotamia, the "land between the rivers," which was so called because it was bounded on one side by the Tigris and on the other by the Euphrates. The overflowing of these rivers was a frequent and serious threat to the people living on that land. Even with our present-day technology, we know all too well how helpless we can be before the forces of unruly water. How much more must have been the terror of the ancient people? This terror is evident in much of their writings. Also found there is the trust that they placed in the god who, they believed, had power over that water and who cared for them in their distress. It is this trust that we find demonstrated in today's readings.

The biblical character Job struggled with the incomprehensibility of the suffering that had befallen him. Why had it happened? He railed against his situation, insisting that he was a righteous man and had done nothing to deserve such a plight. He blamed God, demanding an explanation. When God did reply to Job's complaint, there was no defensiveness, no rebuttal. In fact, God never even mentioned Job's predicament. Instead, there was a spontaneous lesson in cosmology: "Who shut within doors the sea, / when it burst forth from the womb?" In other words, who do you think is responsible for all of this? And, perhaps more to the point, whose power holds it all in balance? Don't you think that the one who has control over the forces of unruly water can support you in your struggle? God is leading Job to realize that the providence that sustains the entire universe also sustains Job within it. The God who speaks to Job is both all-powerful and all-caring.

The same characterization of God is found in the psalm response. In these verses, however, we see that God's power over unruly waters was not merely an accomplished feat of the past, but is an ongoing act in the present. When raging waters engulf individuals, they cry out to God for help. God calms the waves and reaches deep into them in order to rescue those who had been swallowed up. God then carries them to safe harbor where they can praise God for this provident care. To the divine power and care described in the first reading, this psalm reminds us of God's vigilant protection and constant care. It also highlights the appropriate response of praise that we should render to God.

The passage from the gospel does not really contribute any significant characteristic to this understanding of God. What it does is add a human face to it. It depicts Jesus as the one who commands unruly water. Though he appears to be disinterested in the terrifying situation of his disciples, as God seemed to be indifferent to the plight of Job, Jesus is really in control of the waters and he does indeed care for the safety of the other men in the boat. When he calmed the sea, the disciples recognized that Jesus could perform feats that only God could accomplish. In their astonishment they cried out: "Who then is this…?"

Paul had no problem answering this question. He helped his converts to see that Jesus was the one who turned everything upside down. He argued that the unselfishness of Jesus' death gives us the power to live unselfish lives. It was Jesus who inaugurated a new creation in which "the old things have passed away" and "new things have come."

So, what is God like? First, God is all-powerful, and God's power works for us, not against us. Second, God cares for us, and Paul's instruction reveals the lengths to which God will go for our sake. The only appropriate response to such graciousness is thanksgiving and praise.

Praying with Scripture

- How do you envision God? Does your image correspond to the blessings that you have experienced?

- Pray for the grace to trust that you are in God's care, despite the hardships you might have to bear.

- Make the responsorial psalm your prayer today.

THIRTEENTH SUNDAY IN ORDINARY TIME
Readings:
Wis 1:13–15; 2:23–24; Ps 30:2, 4–6, 11–13;
2 Cor 8:7, 9, 13–15; Mark 5:21–43

THE STING OF DEATH

It is always so difficult to deal with the death of another. There is really very little that can ease the pain that cuts so deeply into life. Soothing words and thoughtful gestures may comfort for a time, but then the searing pain returns and we are often left bereft. The sting of death often causes a festering that is not easily healed.

Just what pain do we suffer at the death of another? First, there is the pain of loss. Someone who has been a part of the very fabric of our lives is gone, never to return to it in the same way. Sometimes there is regret that we failed to do or say what might have brought happiness or comfort, or that we said or did that brought anger or caused hurt. There might also be fear and apprehension, for the death of another reminds us that we too are mortal and must face the inevitability of our own death.

Why do we have to die? A traditional understanding traces our death back to the story in Genesis where God warns Adam: "The moment you eat from [the tree of knowledge of good and evil] you are surely doomed to die" (Gen 2:17). Further on, however, we read that the punishment for sin was not death itself, but pain and suffering "until you return to the ground, from which you were taken" (Gen 3:19). This apparent discrepancy points to the complexity of the ancient story, which is really a reinterpretation of several earlier myths that were woven together into a new story. The Israelite version is meant to explain the reality of evil in a world in which everything was created good (Gen 1:4, 10, 12, 18, 21, 25, 31). Evidently, it hasn't done such a good job of explaining, because people continue to ask: "Why does a good God allow bad things to happen to good people?"

Such a question might be more easily answered if we believed, as many ancient religions believed, that there are two warring deities in the world, one responsible for the good and the other responsible for the evil. But we are monotheists who believe that there is only one God, and that God is somehow responsible for everything. Furthermore, we believe that God is good and is concerned with our well-being. Here is precisely where our questions about suffering and death arise again, and our religious tradition struggles to provide answers. These answers might not adequately explain everything; they can only help us live with the mystery and the unanswered questions.

Today's first reading from Wisdom, which seems to reflect the tradition found in Genesis, makes two very interesting claims: "God did not make death"; and "by the envy of the devil, death entered the world." It is clear that these statements do not really reflect accurately the Genesis story, for there God certainly is the origin of death, whether it is understood as a punishment or as the end of suffering. Furthermore, the serpent in the garden is not identified as the devil. Finally, the Genesis story does not mention envy. These differences are later developments and tell us that later generations of believers reformulated the tradition as they continued to struggle with the question of death.

Perhaps we are posing the wrong question. Rather than ask "Why do we die?" we should ask: "How are we to deal with the inevitability of death?" The gospel reading provides insight here. It lays bare the power of Jesus in the face of suffering and death. The ancient people believed that death could come suddenly or progressively. Illness and the debilitation that often accompanied it were considered the onslaught of progressive death. When Jesus healed the woman suffering from hemorrhage, he was really combating the forces of death. The raising of the daughter of the synagogue official was a second demonstration of Jesus' power over death. In each case, faith was required. The woman believed: "If I but touch his clothes, I shall be cured." The official, initially looking for a cure, blindly followed Jesus' instructions even when he was told that his daughter was already dead.

These wonderful stories remind us of Jesus' tenderness toward those who suffer. They might also mislead us, however, if we think that faith will save us from the forces of death. The people in the stories believed that Jesus *could* heal. There was a second disposition at work in them as well. They believed, or trusted, that he *would*. However, neither the woman nor the child was saved from the death that would eventually overtake them.

If we believe that Jesus has power over the forces of death, how do we think he will exercise that power in our lives? Do we trust that we will be spared suffering and death? Or do we place ourselves in his hands, not knowing exactly what will happen, yet trusting in his commitment to our well-being? The ambiguity that surrounds death prompts us to choose the latter option. But do we?

Praying with Scripture

- Do you really believe that Jesus possesses power over the forces of death? If so, can you unreservedly place your life in his hands?

- Pray for the strength to deal with grief at the loss of a loved one and not allow it to overwhelm you.

- Stand faithfully with those who grieve, being a support to them in their grief.

FOURTEENTH SUNDAY IN ORDINARY TIME

Readings:
Ezek 2:2–5; Ps 123:1–4;
2 Cor 12:7–10; Mark 6:1–6

GOD'S GRACE IS SUFFICIENT!

Why do we find it so difficult to accept people who manifest extraordinary talent? Artists, poets, thinkers all tell us that they sometimes feel ostracized when they try to express their creative ideas. Often it is not merely their ideas that are rejected, but also the people themselves. Why is that? Do their remarkable gifts cast shadows on our own unremarkable abilities? Does putting them down lift us up? Or have we convinced ourselves that their difference is merely idiosyncrasy, and our rejection of them is really aimed only at their alleged pride? Whatever the case may be, people who see the world in different and creative ways often have to pay a price for their unusual insight.

Natural talent has been given for the benefit of all. Works of art, pieces of poetry, and profound thoughts are not meant exclusively for those who produce them. They are meant to enhance the lives of us all. Culture and civilization grow out of such remarkable ability. We deprive ourselves of their richness when we reject those blessed with such talent.

The biblical prophets knew what rejection was. Not only did they possess a religious insight that was unique in the community, but this insight was the gift through which God spoke to the people. And the people often rejected both the religious message and the insightful prophet. This was probably because of the way they understood the power of the prophetic word. Since it was considered the word of God, no human could prevent it from accomplishing what it described. If the people did not want to hear that powerful word, their only recourse was to silence the one proclaiming it. Hence prophets often faced persecution and even death.

111

The fate that awaited Ezekiel was no surprise to him. He was informed of it at the time of his call to ministry: "Hard of face and obstinate of heart are they to whom I am sending you." The prophet was here called "son of man," an epithet than means "human being." It was probably a reminder to him of his own human weakness, a weakness, however, that could not hinder the power of the Spirit from working through him. This Spirit would accomplish wonderful deeds. Ezekiel was assured of this: "And whether they heed or resist—for they are a rebellious house–they shall know that a prophet has been among them."

The people of Nazareth to whom Jesus spoke were no better than the ancient Israelites. In fact, they might even have been worse. They rejected Jesus because he was one of their own, a man from Nazareth, someone they had watched grow up. "Where did this man get all this? What kind of wisdom has been given him?" In other words: Who does his think he is? They knew him: "Is he not the carpenter?" The questions that they posed were not simple queries, asked out of interest; they were attacks, issuing from cynical spirits. Because of their hardheartedness and rigid skepticism, Jesus was not able to perform many mighty deeds for these people of his own hometown. They did not possess the faith necessary for miracles to unfold.

This stony reception at the very beginning of Jesus' ministry foreshadowed the kind of rebuffs that lay ahead of him. It must have been particularly stinging, coming from the people of Nazareth, the very people who should have welcomed him with open arms. But they were not welcoming. Rather, "they took offense at him." Jesus simply responded: "A prophet is not without honor except in his native place and among his own kin and in his own house." These words have echoed down through the ages, strengthening others who have offered their religious insights, only to be spurned.

Though Paul too knew rejection, in today's second reading he describes a different obstacle that he had to overcome. He does not claim to have been called as a prophet, but he does acknowledge that he had been blessed with extraordinary revelations. However, he does not take pride in these graces. Instead, he admits that he was also stricken with some kind of ailment, one that he probably found to be somewhat humiliating. He considered this affliction a reminder of his own human weakness and evidence that any success he might experience in ministry was due to the power of God working through him.

Paul had not initially accepted this "thorn in the flesh." Three times he prayed that it might be removed, but to no avail. The answer that he received not only assured him of God's care but, like the words of Jesus above, it has strengthened others who have faced what appeared to be insurmountable obstacles: "My grace is sufficient for you, for power is made perfect in weakness." Today's readings assure us that neither rejection nor personal limitation need inhibit the power of God working in our lives.

Praying with Scripture

- Thank God for the talents that you have been given.

- Have you ever hidden behind a known limitation in order to avoid a challenge? What might you do to correct this?

- Is there someone whose extraordinary abilities have threatened you? Say a prayer of thanksgiving for the gifts bestowed on that person.

FIFTEENTH SUNDAY IN ORDINARY TIME
Readings:
Amos 7:12–15; Ps 85:9–14;
Eph 1:3–14; Mark 6:7–13

WHO? ME?

Last week we reflected on the arduous role of the prophets. We also considered the possibility that we might be called to bear a burden similar to theirs. Today's readings leave no doubt in our minds. In some way, God has indeed called all of us to "prophesy to my people." This might startle us. Us prophets? After all, we are just simple people, engaged in ordinary occupations. We look after our families; we work hard at our jobs; we have all we can do to make ends meet. Few of us have ever been blessed with an extraordinary mystical experience. Some of us are not even particularly "religious." Isn't this idea a bit of a reach? Our first response might be: "Who? Me?" To which God would reply: "Yes, you!"

In the Letter to the Ephesians, Paul is ebullient as he describes the loftiness of their call in Christ. But as Paul speaks to the Ephesians, he is speaking to us as well. He declares that we are all blessed, all chosen, and all destined for adoption by God. We have heard this so often that we might not realize the boldness of this claim. Adoption implies that we have the privileges of a family member, but we also have responsibilities. Paul lists some of the privileges: "redemption by his blood, / the forgiveness of transgressions, / ...wisdom and insight.... / [We] have heard the word of truth, / the gospel of...salvation." These are some of the privileges. Now we must live as redeemed people; we must put aside any transgression; we must make the most of our wisdom and insight; we must proclaim the word of truth to others. These are some of our responsibilities. We might be frightened by such a program and in response declare: "Who? Me?" To which Paul would reply: "Yes, you!"

The gospel reading describes the ministerial activity of the apostles. They were sent out with very few supplies—a reminder that any success that they might achieve would not be attributed to their own doing. In place of material support, they were given authority over unclean spirits and to drive out demons and to heal the sick. Like the apostles, we too have been given authority over unclean spirits. We have been commissioned to preach repentance, to drive out demons, and to cure the sick. Such claims might even startle us more, and we might respond anew: "Who? Me?" To which the disciples would reply: "Yes, you, and you, and you, and every other baptized Christian."

Today's readings reveal once again that God chooses ordinary people and confers on them extraordinary responsibility. Amos was a simple shepherd and a dresser of sycamore trees, yet he was called forth to a prophetic mission and sent to challenge the official priest at the shrine at Bethel. It might have been his unassuming demeanor that prompted Amaziah, the priest of Bethel, to ridicule him with the words: "Off with you, visionary"; go back home; we don't need you here. Many of the apostles were common fishermen, yet they were sent to preach repentance, to heal, and to drive out demons. They went first to the various villages in Galilee, then to Samaria, and finally to the ends of the earth. Paul was an ordinary tentmaker, yet he stood before kings and magistrates, proclaiming the gospel of salvation. Ordinary people are given an extraordinary task so that all will know that the power unleashed through them is really the power of God.

Christians today are mechanics and clerks, teachers and engineers, doctors and housekeepers, politicians and train conductors. Few of them are asked to leave their ordinary trades or professions, for it is precisely within those trades or professions that they fulfill their calling. It is there that they touch minds and hearts and souls with the tenderness of God; and it is there that they heal the people whom they touch. It is there that they instruct and comfort people in need; and it is in that way that they help to drive out the demons that seem to have a stranglehold on those people. In very ordinary ways, these unassuming faithful people participate in the extraordinary establishment of the reign of God.

Perhaps our initial incredulity regarding this extraordinary call stems from the mistaken idea that we cannot do what is required of us, or that we cannot leave the lives we now live. But we can do it, because we have been "blessed…in Christ / with every spiritual blessing in the heavens." With such power, how can we not succeed? Furthermore, most of us do not have to leave the lives that we live. In fact, we probably shouldn't. However, we need only live those lives better, more deeply, more faithfully, with more commitment. We need only discover ways in those lives to proclaim the good news of salvation, to help people release themselves from their addictions, and to touch them with the healing power of God's tenderness. You might still ask: "Who? Me?" To which today's readings reply: "Who else?"

Praying with Scripture

- In what ways might you be a healing presence in the lives of others?

- What message does your life proclaim to others? Is it one of service? Or one of self-preoccupation?

- Reflect on the phrase, "Blessed in Christ with every spiritual blessing in the heavens." How might that phrase embolden you?

SIXTEENTH SUNDAY IN ORDINARY TIME
Readings:
Jer 23:1–6; Ps 23:1–6;
Eph 2:13–18; Mark 6:30–34

TO WHOM SHOULD WE TURN?

The Roman Catholic Church has a long tradition of characterizing its leaders as shepherds. The bishop's or abbot's crosier, despite any ornate decoration that might embellish it, really represents the simple shepherd's crook. This characterization can also be seen in many liturgical prayers and in some theological statements. However, the metaphor originally referred to political leaders, specifically the kings. Archaeology has uncovered many ancient Near Eastern depictions of kings in shepherd garb. This signified the ruler's responsibility to guide and to protect the people of the realm. The hook could gently catch the stray sheep and nudge it back into the flock, while the staff itself could serve as a weapon against threatening animals or poachers. This understanding of the shepherd lies behind today's reading from Jeremiah.

The reading opens with a curse indicting the entire monarchy, which consists of the king and all those who make up the ruling court. These leaders have not simply neglected the people of God; they have actually misled them and caused them to be scattered (probably a reference to the exile.). The shepherds have been occupied with their own advantage rather than with the well-being of the people. Because the people were burdened with false shepherds, God promises to gather them together again as a vigilant shepherd might gather lost sheep and then appoint other shepherds to care for them.

The shepherd theme is further developed in the responsorial psalm, which is probably one of the best-known passages of the Bible. It depicts the gentle and caring features of the shepherd and applies them to God: "The LORD is my shepherd." Though the shepherd is responsible for an entire flock, this psalm reminds us that God is attentive to the needs of the individual, not merely to some impersonal collectivity. The extravagance that characterizes God's solicitude is remarkable. The psalmist is shielded from harm and vindicated in the sight of enemies. A sumptuous meal is prepared, suggesting that this is more than a pastoral scene. Whether the phrase "house of the LORD" is a reference to the temple or merely to a place where God dwells, the fundamental meaning is clear. The psalmist has been under the loving guidance of God and will remain there forever.

The gospel recounts an episode in which Jesus had pity on the crowds. The reason given was that "they were like sheep without a shepherd." As with the reading from Jeremiah, the reference here is probably to religious leaders, for at the time of Jesus, the Jews were an occupied people and the real political power was in the hands of the Romans. Still, just as the earlier Israelite kings, though primarily political leaders, also wielded religious power, so the religious leaders at the time of Jesus also enjoyed significant political influence. The fact that many of them had been co-opted by the Romans was a grave concern for many religious Jews. The gospel writer does not explicitly identify Jesus as a shepherd. However, the shepherd theme is furthered by having Jesus lead his disciples into a deserted place, there to provide them with necessary repose.

At the times of both Jeremiah and Jesus, the people did not strictly separate political and religious leadership, as we do today. Nonetheless, despite the different systems operative, both political and religious leaders still have the responsibility of guiding and protecting the people for whom they are responsible. Ultimately, they exercise their authority as representatives of God who declared: "I myself will pasture my sheep" (Ezek 34:15); or of Jesus who proclaimed: "I am the good shepherd" (John 10:14).

The portrait of Jesus' attentiveness to the needs of others is enhanced by the passage from the Letter to the Ephesians. There he is not only identified as the one who leads us to a peaceful place, but he himself is the peace that reconciles us with each other and with God. The enmity mentioned in the psalm and hinted at in the other readings has been broken down, and the verdant pasture described there is now available to all. But where do we find it? How do we avail ourselves of it?

There are so many people searching today, people hungering for instruction, good people who are looking for direction. They are not unthinking sheep who follow blindly. Rather, they may be parents who are sick with grief over the future of a troubled child; a man stripped of his dignity due to unemployment; a woman facing a pregnancy alone; elderly people who feel that the surge of life in their bodies is gradually diminishing; people who are angry and confused because they have lost confidence in leaders, whether political or religious. They are people who are looking for answers and for meaning. To whom should they turn? God may be our shepherd, but God shepherds us through the agency of other people, not merely the designated leaders, but all of us. Together we have been reconciled with God; together we now make up one body. In some way, we all have the responsibility of leadership.

Praying with Scripture

- What religious leaders have made the most positive impact on your life? How did they do this?

- In what ways do you further the ministry that Jesus bequeathed to the apostles?

- What religious values influence your choice of political leaders? What does this tell you about yourself?

SEVENTEENTH SUNDAY IN ORDINARY TIME

Readings:
2 Kgs 4:42–44; Ps 145:10–11, 15–18;
Eph 4:1–6; John 6:1–15

ENOUGH FOOD TO EAT!

There is so much hunger in the world today. Millions of people go to sleep with empty stomachs. Children are bloated from malnutrition. Wars are fought over food, and people starve as a consequence of its destructive forces. In some corners, there is much political debate about whether or not the earth can actually provide enough food to feed its people. At the same time, farmers in America's breadbasket are often paid subsidies to allow their fields to lie fallow so that the costs of grain can be regulated. In the face of this, populations continue to go hungry. Who will follow the gospel injunction to "feed the hungry"? Where are the needy people to turn for help? At this time of year, when the farmlands of the northern hemisphere look forward to bountiful harvests, the gospels for the next five Sundays contain teaching about the "bread of life." This Sunday's readings focus on the generous power of God that mysteriously meets basic human needs.

In the passages from 2 Kings and the Gospel of John, crowds of people are in need. Not only are these people hungry, but also the food supply is limited and there does not appear to be enough to satisfy their basic needs. It appears that some of them will obviously be sent away with little or no food at all. In both episodes, those responsible for controlling the crowds wonder how the precious food they do have should be distributed. Then, in each instance, in the midst of this need, something extraordinary happens. Enough food is provided, but there is even more available than is required at the moment. How did this happen? And what are we to make of it?

Again and again the versicle of the psalm response answers our questions: "The hand of the Lord feeds us; [God] answers all our needs." Acting through the prophet Elisha, God fed about a hundred people with twenty barley loaves made from the first-fruits of the harvest. It was startling that the prophet directed his servant to give the food to the people, not only because the food would merely satisfy the hunger of a few, but also because the firstfruits of the harvest belonged to God, not to human beings. But the prophet was obeyed, and a miracle unfolded.

The feeding described in the gospel is even more spectacular. Five thousand people had followed Jesus. He had caught their imaginations with the wonders that he had worked. Some of them probably followed him because they hoped to benefit from his miraculous power. Others might have hoped that he was the long-awaited Messiah whose coming had been promised by God. Regardless of their motivation, the people flocked around Jesus. Then, as was the case in the first reading, when it came time to eat, someone stepped forward with a bit of food. This time it was a young man carrying five barley loaves and two fish. Again, like the earlier episode, the people were satisfied, and food was left over. Once again we ask: "How did it happen?"

We may not be able to explain the miracles, but we cannot overlook a very important element in each story, namely, that God works marvels through ordinary people. In the first story, Elisha's servant distributed the food; in the second, Jesus' disciples were the ones who gathered up what was left over after all the people had eaten their fill. Though the miracles did not take place through the power of these individuals, in a sense the events did unfold through the working of their hands. In other words, the stories demonstrate how God meets the needs of people through the services provided by members of the community. Furthermore, those who serve others may not always believe in miracles. The men in these stories certainly did not. They all doubted that the available food would be sufficient: How can I set this before a hundred people? "…but what good are these for so many?" God can and does perform miracles despite our lack of religious imagination.

Paul sketches the profile of the kind of caring community that can work wonders for others. The members will be humble, gentle, and patient, because they belong to the one body and share the same Spirit. As children of the one God who is over all, and in all, and works through all, they will be agents of God's goodwill. We are the community that Paul describes. We are the ones called today to feed the hungry of the world. We cannot allow empty stomachs to cry out in hunger or children to be bloated. We can no longer fight over food, allow the war-torn people to starve, or place economic advantage above basic human need. As members of the body of Christ, we all are diminished whenever any sister or brother goes hungry. However, miracles can unfold through the workings of our own hands. They will happen when we distribute the food destined for all by our generous God.

Prayer with Scripture

- What concrete steps might you take to ensure that others have enough food to eat?

- How willing are you to share what you have with others?

- Pray for the grace to realize that God can accomplish great feats through the very ordinary deeds of your life.

EIGHTEENTH SUNDAY IN ORDINARY TIME
Readings:
*Exod 16:2–4, 12–15; Ps 78:3–4, 23–25, 54;
Eph 4:17, 20–24; John 6:24–35*

BREAD FROM HEAVEN

It is always a challenge to hold in delicate balance our everpressing responsibility to care for ourselves and for others and our humble acknowledgment of our total dependence on God. To admit dependence on anyone, even God, is particularly difficult for people who have the strength and ability to be relatively self-sufficient. We can do things for ourselves and for others all by ourselves, and we prefer not to have to ask for assistance. It may be that we will have to be stripped of our usual sources of ability and support in order to be reminded that our ultimate sustenance comes from God and God alone.

Last Sunday's readings provided us with examples of how those who were hungry are given the food that they need through the unselfish service of other members of the community who mediated God's love and care. This Sunday we look a bit closer at the food itself, which is identified in the first reading and the gospel passage as "bread from heaven." The section from Exodus recounts a fascinating event. After having been delivered by God from Egyptian bondage, the Israelites complain that they have no food. One would think that they would have realized that a God who could perform the wonders they had just experienced would certainly be able to provide them with food, even in the wilderness. One might also presume that their constant complaining would weary God who, as a consequence of their complaining, would lash out at them in anger. But such is not the case. Instead, in response to their grumbling, God supplies them with both meat and "bread."

The "bread" was probably not bread at all. Nor did it come *down* from somewhere, but rather it came *off* something. Most likely it was a substance secreted by the tamarisk tree. This substance hardened as the morning dew evaporated and then deteriorated during the heat of the day. The people, upon seeing it, and not knowing what it was, referred to it as manna (*mān hû,* meaning, "what is it?"). What is important about this bread is not its actual origin or composition, but its meaning. It came from God, and the restrictions for collecting it (only enough for the day) remind us to trust that God will always provide what we need.

The episode reported in the gospel occurred shortly after Jesus had fed the multitude in the wilderness. He knew that the crowd had followed him "not because you saw signs but because you ate the loaves and were filled." Despite their lack of insight into the miracle of the feeding, Jesus took advantage of the moment to teach them a profound lesson. They wanted food; he would give them food. But he would give "food that endures for eternal life." They asked for a sign that would legitimate this bold claim. He had already performed a sign, the miraculous feeding, and yet they demanded another one. Just as God was not wearied by the constant grumbling of the Israelites in the desert, neither was Jesus wearied by the obstinacy of these people. Instead, he further claimed to be the true bread from heaven, declaring: "I am the bread of life; whoever comes to me will never hunger." Here we see Jesus redirecting the people, away from a superficial search for the physical satisfaction that bread can give, to the possibility of access to the deeper things of God. While bread implies eating, it is used here as a metaphor for a different kind of nourishment. The teaching of this section has to do with faith, not Eucharist. Bread of life is a wisdom theme in this section, and those who believe will be satisfied, not those who eat.

Paul insists that acceptance of Jesus as the real source of our lives and the very nourishment of our spirits effects a total transformation in us. So transformed, we are no longer content to live with full bellies but empty minds and hearts. We put aside our old selves steeped in ignorance and self-interest, and we put on a new self, created in Christ's image. Having been fed on the bread from heaven, we are mysteriously transformed into it. The spirit of our minds has been renewed. We have learned Christ; we have been nourished by his teaching. As a result, we launch into a way of living that witnesses to our new understanding, our new life.

What must we do to gain this new life? All we can do is accept it with open and grateful hearts. Today's readings remind us that those sustained by God have not earned such a blessing through their own merit. On the contrary, the Israelites were provided bread from heaven even after they murmured against God. Jesus promised the true bread from heaven to the very people who had been satisfied by the bread he gave them earlier and who were merely looking for more to eat. From this we see that God's generosity is not dependent on our virtue. Rather, it is dependent on God's goodness.

Prayer with Scripture

- How often do you complain when life does not seem to be working out as you hoped or planned? What might you do to remedy this?

- Spend some time today reflecting on the many ways that God has provided for you. Thank God for these blessings.

- In what areas of your life do you still need to be transformed by Jesus who is the "bread of life"?

NINETEENTH SUNDAY IN ORDINARY TIME
Readings:
1 Kgs 19:4–8; Ps 34:2–9;
Eph 4:30—5:2; John 6:41–51

I DOUBT IT!

When we lose faith, it seldom has much to do with mysterious and incomprehensible doctrines like the Trinity, the Hypostatic Union of Jesus Christ, the Immaculate Conception, or the virgin birth. More often, we lose faith in people whom we loved and trusted or to whom we looked for guidance; or we judge life to have taken such a disastrous turn that not even God can remedy the horrendous circumstances in which we find ourselves. In such situations we can lose faith in basic human goodness or in divine providence. And who among us has not been tempted to lose faith? To give up? Even to long for death?

Today's readings provide us with examples of people who doubted despite their having witnessed the incredible power of God. In the passage from 1 Kings, Elijah the prophet had just witnessed God's astounding victory on Mount Carmel. There, the mighty God of Israel had been triumphant over Baal, the powerless deity worshiped by the Canaanites. Elijah should have rejoiced in God's spectacular victory, yet he was cast down by the infidelity of the other Israelites. The prophet had had enough. He had lost faith in his people. He was so dejected that he did not even want to live anymore, and so he asked God to take his life. Despite his loss of faith, God sent an angel to comfort him, to furnish him food and drink. To his credit, Elijah responded positively to God's solicitude—not, however, before he had given up.

In the gospel we read that some of those who had just witnessed Jesus' ability to supply them with food turned away when he explained the source of his mysterious power. They too had had enough, not of bread, but of Jesus' bold claim to be the "bread that came down from heaven." After all, they knew who he was; they were familiar with his family. They knew that he came from the insignificant town of Nazareth, not from heaven. What had gotten into him to make such outlandish claims? Their response to those claims must have been something like: "I doubt it!"

The final theme of the gospel reading is both striking and ambiguous. Jesus said that the real bread from heaven was not the manna that God sent to feed their ancestors in the desert, but his own flesh—a likely allusion here to the Eucharist. However, the word *flesh* could also refer to the human manner of his being in the world. To give his flesh means that he will surrender his own human life so that the world might have eternal life. Thus we see that the Eucharist and the death of Jesus cannot be separated. This final statement merely compounded their incredulity. First he accused the people of murmuring; then he stated that not all of them had experienced God; finally he insisted that he is the source of eternal life. Is it any wonder that those who had gathered in the hope of being given more bread should be astonished at the assertions he is making? We should not be surprised if some of them exclaimed: "I doubt it!"

In some ways it is much easier to study the teachings of the faith than it is to live by them. Perhaps this is because we are not expected to understand fully the mysteries but to pledge our allegiance to the divine mystery. We are expected to live in a faithful manner through the mysterious and often agonizing twists and turns of life. We all have to live with a measure of disappointment, loss, and failure, and yet not give up on other people or on God. We all have to allow our expectations and cherished points of view to be challenged, and yet not turn our backs on the possibility of new insight. We all have to be willing to endure hardship without being overwhelmed by it or sacrificing our spirits on the altar of its cruel intensity. The faith or trust of all of us will be tested often during our lifetime. As disturbing as that testing might be, it can also be a time of strengthening and deepening rather than doubting. Many who persist in trusting God come to acknowledge that somehow, even mysteriously, God's gentle presence has been guiding them all the way.

Today Paul provides us with a plan of action. He urges us to do away with bitterness, fury, and anger. It will only deepen our resentment and add to the burden that we are already carrying. Instead, we are called to "be imitators of God, as beloved children, and [to] live in love." We are to live lives of kindness, compassion, and forgiveness. And what has any of this to do with faith? Everything! For it is faith that strengthens us to live in this new way in a world filled with terror and violence, in a church often marked by betrayal and disillusionment, and in families that may nurture long-standing animosity. Will we ever really understand our faith? I doubt it! Will we ever really learn to live by it? I hope so!

Prayer with Scripture

- Read today's responsorial psalm slowly, asking God to deepen your trust in God's loving care for you.

- In what ways might you be a support to others when they are going through difficult times?

- How open are you to new religious insights?

TWENTIETH SUNDAY IN ORDINARY TIME
Readings:
Prov 9:1–6; Ps 34:2–7;
Eph 5:15–20; John 6:51–58

YOU ARE KINDLY INVITED...

It is so easy to get a meal nowadays. You don't have to "waste" time shopping for food and then preparing it, setting the table, and cleaning up afterward. All you have to do is make a stop at one of the convenient fast food restaurants. Once there, you don't even have to actually enter the confines. All you have to do is sit in the car, place an order at a small metal voice box, drive a short distance around the building, make your payment, and food is handed to you, all prepared, hot, and ready to eat. But things are quite different when you are invited to a banquet. In such a situation, you may not have to prepare the food, but you certainly have to get yourself ready. You will be very concerned about your appearance. You may even want to purchase new clothes for the evening, because a banquet is usually a memorable event.

When you are invited to a banquet, you seldom ask about the menu, nor are you generally consulted about your personal preferences. If it is a genuine banquet, you presume that the food will be of high quality, expertly prepared, and appetizingly presented. Besides, the point of many banquets is not the character or quantity of the food served, though these certainly are important. Rather, it is the significance of the event, the importance of the host, and the status of the honored guests.

Today's readings invite us to two banquets. The first comes from the Wisdom tradition of ancient Israel. Wisdom, personified as a woman, spreads out a sumptuous banquet to which she invites "whoever is simple...the one who lacks understanding." The dressed meat and mixed wine that she offers are really insight and understanding, and one would be a fool to turn down her invitation. Still, this is an invitation to accept what is freely given; it is not a command. Nor is it a reward for those who are deserving of it. Woman Wisdom seeks those who are not wise so that she can offer them the riches of wisdom that she possesses.

In the gospel reading we see that Jesus too spreads a banquet. In this part of his discourse, the bread of which he speaks is clearly eucharistic: "For my flesh is true food, and my blood is true drink." His body, not merely his teaching, is the true bread that came down from heaven. As was the case in the passage from Wisdom, this banquet is not for those who are deserving of it. In fact, some of those in the crowd that had gathered around him, to whom the invitation had been extended, not only refused it, but also challenged its legitimacy: "How can this man give us his flesh to eat?" Just as the fare of Wisdom's banquet metaphorically stood for a reality much deeper than meat and wine, so the food that Jesus offered was much more than simple bread. He offered them, and us, his flesh for the life of the world. Anyone who might turn down his invitation would be more than a fool; such a person would be rejecting life itself.

The wisdom theme is found in the second reading as well. Paul warns against foolish living and counsels wisdom. His words of warning are startling: "The days are evil." Some of the evils he warned against are with us still, evils such as drunkenness and debauchery. Though we might be inclined to overlook such behavior, it obviously presents obstacles to a life lived wisely. However, there are other evils that may not be as apparent. In fact, they may not even be considered evil. There is the national or religious arrogance that presumes that our point of view is the only legitimate one; there is the abuse of power that denies the more vulnerable individuals or groups the self-determination that is rightfully theirs; there is the personal or corporate greed that deprives whole societies of the necessities of life; there is the glorification of violence that destroys both the victim and the perpetrator. Paul could easily say to us as well: "The days are evil."

Despite the fact that we have all been invited to be enriched at Woman Wisdom's table and to be transformed by the body and blood of Jesus, there are times when we prefer the fast food of a life of complacency. We would rather stay comfortably in the lives that we have fashioned for ourselves than have to go through all of the trouble required of reform or renewal. We are satisfied to continue in ignorance. It has served us to this point, so "why fix it if it ain't broke?" Why? Because ignorance is not bliss; because we cannot long survive on the fare of foolishness or obstinacy; because whoever eats the body of the Lord and drinks his blood will live forever—and we are all kindly invited.

Praying with Scripture

- What personal makeover might be necessary to prepare you for the banquet to which you have been invited?

- What, in your mind, are the evils of our day? How do you deal with their temptation? What do you do to remedy them?

- Though eucharistic devotion has waned in recent years, how can you deepen it within yourself?

TWENTY-FIRST SUNDAY IN ORDINARY TIME
Readings:
Josh 24:1–2a, 15–17, 18b;
Ps 34:2–3, 16–21; Eph 5:21–32; John 6:60–69

To Whom Shall We Go?

The readings for today all call for difficult decisions. The people at the time of Joshua had to decide which god they would worship. Would it be the God of their ancestors who had cared for them through difficult times, but who also made great demands on them? Or would it be the local god, one who seemed to be able to provide its devotees with prosperity? The way this account was written suggests that the choice was an easy one. God had provided for them in the past, and so they seemed confident that God would continue to provide for them in the future. However, the circumstances of life had changed for them. The God who had brought them out of Egyptian bondage was a warrior-God, one who could accomplish feats with an "outstretched arm" (Exod 6:6). In this new country they would be faced with all of the challenges of agriculture, and that was the realm claimed by the gods of the Amorites. There was no guarantee that the God of Israel had power over those forces of nature, and yet they chose to serve that God.

Though many today will not be happy with the marital roles described by Paul, what he was proposing for his converts was really revolutionary for that day. In line with the customs of the patriarchal society of the time, he counseled wives to be subject to their husbands. However, he also directed husbands to love their wives as they loved themselves. Even more revolutionary was the

THE WORD FOR EVERY SEASON

model against which husbands were to measure their love. It was the self-sacrificing love that Christ had for the church. If such unselfish love was practiced in marriages, it would go a long way toward dismantling some of the oppressive structures of patriarchal hierarchy. The challenge was placed before the new Christians; we have no idea whether or not they chose to accept it.

It is clear from the gospels that Jesus was not the kind of Messiah that many people were expecting. Most likely it was easy to follow him when he performed great feats of healing, or when he stood against rigid religious leaders in defense of the marginalized and despised. However, he did not always receive warm acceptance from his audience. Today's gospel reading demonstrates this. His discourse on "the bread of life" (sections of which have been the gospel readings the past few Sundays) made great demands on his hearers. Even many of his disciples said: "This saying is hard; who can accept it?" Some of them were so upset by it that they left him and returned home disappointed. Many people might be surprised by the fact that Jesus allowed them to leave and did not follow after them, begging them to come back. Hard as it might have been, this was their decision, and he gave them the freedom to make it.

Making the decision for God is no easier today then it was at the time of Joshua, or that of Jesus or of Paul. Alternatives are often so much more appealing. In some situations we are attracted to success, or we want to be like others. Some of the religious values of the past might seem outmoded. Or, social pressures could be so strong that we might prefer the status quo. We might convince ourselves that circumstances have worked well up to now. Why change them? Why unsettle the waters? But then we are confronted by a call to alter our understanding of God, a call that might demand a significant change in our thinking and in the way we live and interact with others.

All such decisions would be hard enough if people were sure that in making them they were deciding rightly, but that is not always the case. How could the people of Joshua's time or Paul's Christians or the followers of Jesus have been absolutely sure that their decision was the right one? They couldn't. They had to trust in Joshua or Paul or Jesus. Ultimately, they were trusting that God would not lead them astray.

And what of us? We must believe that our religious tradition can carry us into new situations, and that its values can continue to be vital despite the new challenges we find there. At the same time, we must be willing to let go of perspectives or practices that no longer serve people well, perspectives or practices that we now realize diminish rather than enhance life. Finally, our understanding of God must grow and change, as we do. We get new insights, not only from teachers or preachers, but from the experiences of life itself. We see genuine holiness in people of other faiths; we ourselves are willing to sacrifice for the sake of others; God no longer seems remote or committed only to one people. These are hard sayings; who can accept them? Jesus asked: "Do you also want to leave?" Will we be able to reply with Simon Peter: "To whom shall we go? You have the words of eternal life."

Praying with Scripture

- How open are you to the new situations and new insights that God places in your path?

- Do you cling tenaciously to what is familiar, or do you trust God enough to step into the unknown?

- Pray for the insight to recognize God's will in the specific decisions of your life and for the courage to follow it regardless of the cost.

TWENTY-SECOND SUNDAY IN ORDINARY TIME

Readings:
Deut 4:1–2, 6–8; Ps 15:2–5;
Jas 1:17–18, 21b–22, 27;
Mark 7:1–8, 14–15, 21–23

THE POWER OF WORDS

Children sing-song the ditty: "Sticks and stones can break my bones, but names can never hurt me." How wrong this little claim really is! Broken bones will mend, but we do not always recover from cruel words. In fact, the words of others can sometimes prevent us from becoming the best we might be. Though this may be particularly the case when we are vulnerable because of youth or inexperience, it can be true at any or all periods of life. At times of anger or insensitivity, we might use words as weapons against others. We might slander them or reveal a truth that could ruin their reputation. However, the opposite can be true as well. There are words that are healing and encouraging. Another's words "You're not alone; I'm here" can do wonders when we feel bereft of support. Words of affection or love strengthen and transform us. The simple phrase "I love you" can turn life from black and white to Technicolor. There is definitely power in words.

In the Jewish tradition, the Ten Commandments, frequently referred to as the "ten words," have power as well. Unfortunately, many of us today view these laws as restrictions on life. The Israelites certainly did not. They believed that these words, delivered to them through Moses at the time of the making of the covenant, were the words of God. They were powerful because they expressed God's will for them. They viewed the Ten Commandments as helpful guides for living lives of wisdom and truth, generosity and social harmony. They cherished these laws because they believed that following them was the way they would live out their covenant relationship with God. If we look carefully at these ordinances, we will see that they sketch a picture of a God who is committed to justice. The God behind this set of laws requires that people both show the proper reverence toward God and live honorably in society, respecting each other's person and property. Understood in this way, we can see why they considered the Ten Commandments words of life. Finally, the life that they would live as they followed these counsels would be a witness to the other nations: "What great nation has statutes and decrees that are as just as this whole law?"

The author of the Letter of James uses an agricultural image to speak about the power of the word, specifically the word of truth. He is no doubt referring to the word of the gospel, the word that has been planted in us, the word through which we are reborn in baptism. He insists that it is not enough to hear that word and claim allegiance to it. It must also bring forth fruit; that word must be allowed to transform our lives, for this is the way that we will live out our covenant with God. Once again we see that the word is not hollow. It is pregnant with life, and when it takes root and blossoms in the lives of believers, it will give witness to the goodness and power of God. The psalm response gives us a glimpse of such a way of living. God's words will bring forth blamelessness and justice, thoughtfulness and honesty in dealing with others. These are certainly words of truth.

There are times when strict adherence to the law can also produce the opposite of what it was intended to effect. Rather than enhance human life and direct us to God, rigid conformity can restrict life and result in smug self-satisfaction. In the gospel story, Jesus chides those who demand unyielding observance of simple customs that grew up in an attempt to safeguard the law but were now considered as important as the law itself. Because he makes exceptions when the good of others seems to call for them, Jesus is accused of serious violation of God's law. Though he does at times set the law aside, he nonetheless respects it. He argues that the "ten words" are meant to be guides, not shackles, and he insists that adherence out of an empty sense of duty is not enough. They may criticize what they consider his lack of obedience to the law, but he criticizes their hollow observance of it.

The passage from Isaiah that Jesus quotes sums up his perspective regarding the words of the law: "*This people honors me with their lips, / but their hearts are far from me"* (Mark 7:6; see also Isa 29:13). Nowhere does Jesus suggest that the practice of religion is unimportant. Rather, he insists that external practice, whether it is of worship or of teaching, must be informed by the right dispositions of the heart. It is these dispositions that generate true devotion. It is these dispositions that determine whether or not we are truly religious or simply observant. Furthermore, it is out of these dispositions that our words spring, for as Jesus remarks, what defiles does not come from outside of us, but from deep within us. Commitment to the Ten Commandments must spring from the heart. Only then will they be words of genuine truth and life.

Praying with Scripture

- Examine your customary language. Is it life-giving and gentle, or is it sharp and hurtful?

- Spend some time in reflection on the Ten Commandments. How do they direct you to live an honorable life?

- Pray that God will bless us with people who can honestly and faithfully help us interpret our religious tradition for us today.

TWENTY-THIRD SUNDAY IN ORDINARY TIME
Readings:
Isa 35:4–7a; Ps 146:7–10; Jas 2:1–5; Mark 7:31–37

BACK TO THE PRESENT

In the movie *Back to the Future,* an enterprising character portrayed by Michael J. Fox conspires with a brilliant, eccentric scientist to drive a transformed Delorean into the past in order to do something that will change the present. It is a delightful farce with both humor and suspense. In the end, the hero is left with an appreciation of his present life. The readings for this Sunday invite us to move through time, but in the opposite direction. They have a clear eschatological or future focus. In other words, rather than look to the past for the sake of the present, they have us look to the future—but still for the sake of the present.

In the oracle of salvation taken from the Book of Isaiah, God promises to come with healing and blessings. Those who are in any way prevented from living life to the fullest will be freed from impediments and will sing and dance with joy. The life-giving water promised symbolizes whatever is needed to achieve this peace and fullness. Though the standards by which we live may differ one from another, this is the kind of future for which we all yearn.

In the gospel account, we see Jesus fulfilling the promise that God made. His ministry establishes God's reign in which healing and the blessings of life are no longer merely expectations of the future. Through the power of Jesus, they unfold before our very eyes, or at least before the eyes of those who witness Jesus' wondrous deeds. The future is now in the present, and it did not arrive in the wake of some delightful science-fiction farce. This future is real, even though one needs eyes of faith to recognize it. The responsorial psalm picks up the theme found in these two readings. As we pray it, we rejoice that God's promise for peace and fullness of life has been kept. God has indeed removed the obstacles that diminish life. We rejoice because "the God of Jacob keeps faith forever."

No one would dare suggest that these two readings and psalm response picture situations as fanciful as those produced by Hollywood. However, unless we too can step into the mysterious future that they envision, they will remain simply religious stories, and we will sit in the audience watching someone else's drama unfold. But how do we take that step into the future?

The author of the Letter of James offers an example of how this can be done. He describes a situation with which we are all only too familiar. Who of us has not been impressed when a fashionably dressed woman or man joins our gathering? If this is a person of renown, we might fall all over ourselves showing deference. "Sit here; you can see better. Can I get you something to drink?" Do we show that same kind of courtesy to those among us who are less fortunate or well known? Is the one who answers the phone less significant than the one who pays the salary?

James insists: "Show no partiality." In a society like ours, where we dote on people who have money or power or celebrity, this mandate is countercultural. We cannot deny that there are differences in social status. If we show respect to all people regardless of the differences, however, treating them as children of God, we will be taking a step into that future of peace and blessing. In a very real sense, that future will be made present.

As stated above, we look to the future for the sake of the present. This is not the same as living in the future because the present is too painful or just plain boring. Nor is it the same as planning the future, which seems to be a favorite pastime of many people. The future referred to in these readings is not simply the one we want for ourselves. It is God's future, the one that God wants for us. This is the future depicted in God's promises, the future in which we will be freed from whatever prevents us from living life to the full.

Though it is God's future, it does not simply dawn upon us one day. In a very real sense, this future, which is really the reign of God, takes shape when we make a decision to live God's promises in the present. God holds out the possibility of this future, but we must decide to step into it.

The psalm offers other examples of how we might step into that future. It will dawn upon us when we work to ensure justice for those oppressed, food for those who are hungry, freedom for those unjustly held captive, sight to those who cannot see, relief to those crushed by life, protection to widows and orphans, and respect to strangers. This is the future promised by God, and each time we accomplish such feats we bring God's future "back to the present."

Praying with Scripture

- Who do you know that has brought peace and fullness to the world? What did they do?

- How might you bring the future of peace and fulfillment into the present?

- Go out of your way to show respect to someone who is normally overlooked or disdained.

TWENTY-FOURTH SUNDAY IN ORDINARY TIME
Readings:
Isa 50:5–9a; Ps 116:1–6, 8–9;
Jas 2:14–18; Mark 8:27–35

WHAT DID YOU EXPECT?

I'm sure that I'm not the only one who, more than once, has wondered—"What was Jesus really like?" I know what the gospels say. But they are theological testimonies that reflect the concerns of the respective Christian communities that produced them, not impartial reports. I know that he went about the countryside, into the villages and cities preaching and healing; I know that he made friends that hung on his every word and marveled at his power, as well as enemies who resented his audacity and his popularity among the people. But what was he really like? I'm sure that through the years I have fashioned an image of him out of what I have learned from our religious tradition and from my own expectations. As pivotal as this image may be in directing my own Christian behavior, I am sure that it is far from the historical reality.

Just as we wonder, "What was he like?" so the people of Israel wondered, "What will he be like?" They too had ideas about the one whom God would send to inaugurate the time of fulfillment. Since they had always looked to the king for leadership, it is understandable that they would presume that this future leader would be an anointed king. Their priests were also leaders, and so some thought that he would be an anointed priest. This explains why the people referred to this future leader as the "anointed one," or Messiah *(māshîah)*. The people's disappointment with both the monarchy and the priesthood prompted them to look outside of human institutions for the long-expected leader. They believed that God would send someone from heaven itself ("One like a son of man," Dan 7:13). Another very early tradition records a promise made to Moses: "I will raise up for them a prophet like you from among their kinsmen" (Deut 18:18). What did they hope he would be like? By the time of Jesus, there were many very different messianic traditions.

The array of messianic traditions serves as the backdrop for today's gospel reading in which Jesus asks, "Who do people say that I am?" In response, the disciples list a few of the more popular traditions. The fact that the people thought of him as messianic should be noted. However, each tradition included specific expectations. Would Jesus fulfill them? The passage mentions neither the royal nor the priestly tradition, thus disregarding anticipation of political or cultic reform. Some people thought that Jesus might be Elijah, the mysterious prophet, whose return, they believed, would herald the advent of the reign of God (Mal 3:23). Others regarded him as John the Baptist come back to life. Jesus asked his disciples: "But who do you say that I am?" Without referring to any specific tradition, Peter simply replied: "You are the Christ," the Greek word for *anointed one* or *messiah*.

Jesus himself tells us within which messianic expectation we are to understand him. He is not a political leader as the royal tradition might suggest. Nor is he a member of the priestly establishment. He is indeed the Son of Man, the mysterious one sent by God from heaven. To this tradition, however, Jesus adds a startling dimension, that of suffering and persecution. He announces that he will be rejected and ultimately killed. How can this be? The people have been waiting, longing for a messiah. Why, when he finally comes, would they put him to death? The answer is quite simple, though tragic: he did not meet their expectations.

After the early Christians began to grasp the meaning of Jesus' death and resurrection, they perceived the tradition of the "suffering servant" as a foreshadowing of his suffering. Today, when we read the passage from Isaiah, it is very easy for us to understand why they did. Both the servant and Jesus were disgraced, beaten, and spat upon. Despite such treatment, they did not rebel. Both placed their trust in God, believing that they were to be vindicated. However, such understanding of Jesus' messianic character was recognized only after his resurrection. During his lifetime, not even his closest companions understood. Add to this misunderstanding Jesus' directive that those who wish to follow him must follow him in his suffering as well as in his preaching and healing, and the disappointment of his hearers is compounded.

What do we expect today? So many people seem to think that God is just waiting to swoop down and save us from peril, and they are very disillusioned when this does not happen. The second reading, often misunderstood as a contradiction of Paul's teaching of "faith alone," insists that "faith of itself, if it does not have works, is dead." In other words, our lives must demonstrate what we believe. And if we believe that Jesus has in fact already inaugurated the reign of God, our lives must demonstrate this. We must be living evidence of this reign. He came as the one sent by God; he was rejected because he did not meet their expectations. Will we follow their example? Or will we accept the kind of Messiah he was and follow him?

Praying with Scripture

- What about the character of Jesus' messiahship do you find most challenging? Why?

- Decide on one or two concrete ways that you might make your faith a concrete example of the reign of God.

- Pray for the grace to see how the sufferings in your life might be a way of following in the footsteps of Jesus.

TWENTY-FIFTH SUNDAY IN ORDINARY TIME

Readings:
*Wis 2:12, 17–20; Ps 54:3–8;
Jas 3:16—4:3; Mark 9:30–37*

THE WAY OF THE WISE

There seem to be contradictions in the messages found in today's readings. James teaches that the way of righteousness leads to peace, while the author of Wisdom describes a conspiracy plotted against a righteous one. In the gospel, Jesus first informs his disciples that he will be the victim of just such a conspiracy, and then he subverts their standard for judging importance. What are we to make of this?

Any wisdom tradition is based on some form of the theory of retribution: good or wise behavior brings forth success; wicked or foolish behavior yields misfortune. Wisdom teaching itself is a collection of maxims gleaned from experience, each providing a vignette exemplifying this theory. Though this tradition offers a high ideal, its teaching is not unrealistic. The sages knew that those who choose the way of righteousness might be confronted with obstacles that seem insurmountable. The reading from the Book of Wisdom describes such a situation. People who try to live lives of integrity are not always appreciated. In fact, they are often ridiculed and sometimes even persecuted. Their very lives can act as a rebuke of the lives of others, their goodness an accusation. There are people who seem to take delight in pushing decent individuals to their limits, trying to show that they are no better than the rest. If they cannot corrupt these good people, they try instead to get rid of them.

The Letter of James describes several situations that we all know so well. Jealousy and selfishness do indeed spawn disorder as we witness in so many scandals of our day. We also know that desiring the land or natural resources of other nations often leads to war. If we are honest, we will admit that only when we learn to bridle our inordinate passions will we experience true wisdom that is "peaceable, gentle, compliant, full of mercy." The ideal that James offers is not beyond our reach. We have already tasted the kind of life he sketches. We have known happiness and satisfaction in our families and communities. We know from experience that certain options are set before us, and we have decided to choose the path leading to peace.

Jesus is the ultimate example of the victimization referred to in the first reading. He was the righteous one par excellence. When those who opposed him were unable to undermine the success of his ministry, they plotted to get rid of him. He knew it, and yet he was not deterred. In this he became the model par excellence of how one should continue faithfully on the path of righteousness despite immense obstacles, leaving the outcome in God's hands.

We all try to fashion our lives and our world for ourselves and for our children so that the ideal presented by James might become a reality. But one does not have to live long to realize that the other scenario too often forces itself upon us. The people upon whom we relied seem to betray us; unbridled violence locks us in a state of terror; hatred and crime victimize whole populations. Goodness does not guarantee success and happiness, and shameless behavior sometimes seems to win out. When we are caught in the throes of such peril, we ourselves might question the value of clinging to our noble standards. Once again a choice is set before us. Will we discover that our integrity is nothing but a veneer? Will we succumb to the temptations of the "low road"? Or will our trust in God carry us through? Will we choose the "high road" of loyal discipleship despite the cost that this may exact?

The gospel reading ends on what appears to be a strange note. After Jesus reveals the tragic end that he faces, the disciples argue about their own status within the community. Hadn't they been listening to him? In response to their quarreling, Jesus' words turn their, and our, expectations upside down: The greatest becomes the least; the first becomes the last. He insists that it is in receiving society's most vulnerable that we receive Jesus himself, and in receiving him, we receive God. *This* is the epitome of true wisdom.

On second glance, the messages found within these readings are not contradictory after all. Wisdom urges us to choose the right path. Jesus gives us a glimpse of the character of that path, namely, embracing the vulnerable in our midst—the defenseless children, the despairing poor, the terrified mentally ill, the marginalized disabled, the refugees of war. The vulnerable are all around us. The world seems to say: "Get out of life what you can. Let others take care of themselves." The disciple of Jesus says: "How can I help?" This is foolish in the eyes of some, and they may ridicule and even persecute those who follow this way. But it is the way of the wise, and the fruit of such righteousness is true peace.

Praying with Scripture

- Consider the times in your life when you experienced deep peace and contentment. How was this the consequence of making right choices?

- Consider the times when you suffered because of the right choices you made. Are you satisfied with the way you responded?

- Who are the vulnerable in your life, and how might you be more helpful to them?

TWENTY-SIXTH SUNDAY IN ORDINARY TIME
Readings:
Num 11:25–29; Ps 19:8, 10, 12–14;
Jas 5:1–6; Mark 9:38–43, 45, 47–48

THE RIGHT STUFF

Anyone hungry for a heated discussion need only raise the topic of criteria for acceptance in church ministry today. Before we know it, we will be deluged with complicated issues such as lay ministry, women's ordination, celibate priesthood, homosexual candidates, to name but a few. Such issues can hardly be resolved in a short reflection. But neither can they be ignored when the readings for the day actually raise the question of suitability for ministry. The readings force the question: "Who has the right stuff?" Perhaps a better question is: "What *is* the right stuff?"

The reading from Numbers illustrates two important criteria for religious service, namely, selection by God and community confirmation. Both were important. One did not simply assume the role of prophet; one was called to it; the Spirit of God was bestowed upon the one called to prophesy. On the other hand, the prophetic role was always exercised within the community for the sake of the community, not as an individual prerogative. Things seemed to work when both criteria were present. As the reading demonstrates, however, tensions arose when a necessary criterion was missing. Moses, the recognized religious leader, did not say that community confirmation was irrelevant. Rather, he questioned Joshua's reason for opposing Eldad and Medad. Was Joshua really defending Moses' authority? Or was he trying to exercise control over prophetic selection? The reading itself does not tell us. Instead, it leaves us with unanswered questions.

We should be careful not to use the reading from Numbers to champion one side of a contemporary issue over the other. Still, though it recounts an ancient situation, it does provide some insights that might help us today. It shows that the prophetic call came from God, and while the community (not just community leadership) played an important role in determining this ministry, it could not control the activity of God's Spirit. The community was challenged to be faithful to its religious tradition, while at the same time open to new ways that God provided for the people.

In the gospel reading, the community expectation is quite similar. Only recognized disciples were thought to have the authority to minister. Like Moses in the first reading, Jesus challenged a rigid understanding of ministerial legitimacy. He pointed to commitment to the service of others in his name as the paramount criterion for ministry, insisting that "whoever is not against us is for us." In other words, circumstances can change the criteria used for judging suitability. Here, too, community authority is upheld, while the need to be open to new ways that God may be calling others is placed firmly before us.

An unrelated theme is found in the Letter of James. By means of a prophetic pronouncement of doom, the wealthy are condemned for having hoarded the treasures of the earth. Preoccupied with their own comfort, they ignored the needs of others. They were busy amassing money rather than sharing it with the poor. While the reading itself condemns these selfish people, from the perspective of today's focus on ministry we can draw a sharp contrast between these wealthy and those in the gospel who give a cup of water to those who belong to Christ. In this way, another criterion for ministry becomes clear, that is, unselfish service of those in need.

The second part of the gospel is a warning against giving scandal. The Greek word translated "cause to sin" (cf. Mark 9:42) really means "cause to stumble or be scandalized." While many commentators believe that the "little ones" of whom Jesus speaks are children, others maintain that since the entire passage speaks of following Jesus, the reference here is to disciples. They are, after all, children of God, and in this same gospel, Jesus does call his disciples "children" (Mark 10:24). Whatever the reference, Jesus warns against causing another to stumble or be scandalized.

Just what is the scandal in the question of ministry in the church today? Is it that people who do not conform to customary patterns are disregarding the authority of the tradition and are audaciously stepping forward to assume ministerial responsibilities? Is it the fact that members of the church, both those who are in leadership positions and those who are not, are insensitive to the prompting of the Spirit and insist that the church continue to do things the way they have always been done? Or might it be a bit of both?

When in the throes of such a struggle, it is difficult to have a clear perspective. It is much easier to cling tenaciously to one's own position on the matter. Today's readings remind us that there are important values to preserve on both sides of the issue. They also clearly point to the core of the matter, namely, the genuine needs of God's people. Together, as a community, we must discover how these needs can best be served, and we must discover this while being faithful both to the authentic tradition and to the mysterious ever-present Spirit of God.

Praying with Scripture

- Read the responsorial psalm prayerfully, reflecting on the value of a sound and enduring religious tradition.

- Pray for openness to the Spirit of God that is moving through the church in new and mysterious ways.

- Resolve to perform one act of service that you may never have performed before.

TWENTY-SEVENTH SUNDAY IN ORDINARY TIME
Readings:
Gen 2:18–24; Ps 128:1–6;
Heb 2:9–11; Mark 10:2–16

WE CAN'T REALLY LIVE ALONE

"It is not good for the man to be alone," writes the author of Genesis. Nor is it good for the woman or the child. Our fundamental human need to bond with another is beyond question. We are told that newborns may die if they do not experience human touch. And even if they do not die, they may be psychologically scarred for life. Our identity, our sense of worth, and the character of our maturity are all shaped by the quality of our deep bonds with significant others.

The creation story from which today's reading is taken, as poetic in form as it may be, shows that the ancient Israelites were clearly aware of the importance of being joined one to another. The woman is made of the very substance of the man, bone of his bone, flesh of his flesh. Contrary to what some have believed, being made from a part of him does not make her inferior to him any more than the man formed from the substance of the earth is considered inferior to the earth. Rather, the character of her ori-

145

gin makes her one with him. They are bonded. She is a suitable partner (a much better rendering of the Hebrew word *ezer* than is the common translation *helper*).

The woman and the man are bonded on several levels. They are of the same bone and flesh. In other words, they are equally human beings. But bone and flesh can be understood figuratively as well. Bone stands for strength and flesh stands for weakness, and together they encompass the entire range of human characteristics (much like A to Z includes all letters of the alphabet). It is because of this more comprehensive bonding that they are suitable partners. The most obvious expression of this bonding is marriage and the creation of a new family unit.

Marital bonding is a theme in the gospel as well. Jewish law allowed divorce, and so the Pharisees' questioning of Jesus was not a search for information. They were trying to trick him, to see if he would criticize the Mosaic tradition and thus place himself at odds with the people. Jesus was not caught in their trap; he did not find fault with Moses. Instead he acknowledged the tenuous nature of human bonding, and he pointed to divorce as a concession. He then reminded his hearers of the bond established between woman and man as found in the Genesis account.

Whether or not one agrees that in some situations divorce should be granted, one cannot but be saddened at the high instance of its occurrence. In some cases of divorce, the marital bond is severed; in others it may never really have been forged. Too often the bond does not even seem to be a serious consideration. This is tragic, not simply because divorce violates a precept of the church, but because it lays bare the absence of a form of bonding that is so essential for human fulfillment and happiness.

The psalm response expands the marital theme to include the children born of the union. This raises the issue of another kind of bonding, the bonding of generations. Each of us is a link between the past and the future. As parents bond with children, they hand on the heritage of the past; as children bond with parents, they open up to them the possibilities of the future. Children enrich our lives "like olive plants / around your table." No wonder the psalmist prays: "May you see your children's children." They are our way of looking into the future. And the way we bond with them is our way of influencing that future.

The gospel's picture of Jesus surrounded by children is so familiar to us that we may not realize how extraordinary it really is. In ancient Near Eastern cultures, children belonged to the world of women, not to that of men. In the Bible, along with women and resident aliens, children generally represented vulnerability. Thus, Jesus is depicted as welcoming them not only because they are endearing but also because they are vulnerable and in need of the protection of others. Then, as so often happens, he turns our perceptions inside out. The child, dependent on others for nurture and protection, is set before us as an example of how we are to stand before God—open and trusting.

The final example of bonding can be seen in the reading from the Letter to the Hebrews. Jesus became one of us, bone of our bone and flesh of our flesh. As one of us, he "[tasted] death for everyone." He was not only the sacrifice, but also the high priest. Thus the writer could say: "He who consecrates and those who are being consecrated all have one origin." We are now his sisters and brothers, bonded with him, and through him bonded with God. We are really not alone.

Praying with Scripture

- Consider the ways in which you are bonded with others. What might you do to strengthen those bonds?

- Reflect on bonds that have been broken. What might you have done better?

- Pray for a deepened realization of what it means to be a child of God.

TWENTY-EIGHTH SUNDAY IN ORDINARY TIME

Readings:
Wis 7:7–11; Ps 90:12–17;
Heb 4:12–13; Mark 10:17–30

CHOOSE LIFE!

A passage in Deuteronomy recounts Moses' last words to the Israelites: "I have set before you life and death, the blessing and the curse. Choose life" (30:19). While it is a stark admonition, it is also rather curious. The choice seems so obvious. Who would choose death over life? Today's readings offer us a similar kind of choice. For the author of Wisdom, it is between wisdom and the trappings of royalty; for the man in the gospel who came to Jesus, it is between renunciation and possessions. For both, the choice is just as stark as it was for the Israelites. It is not at all curious, however, for the options are clearly delineated.

In the first reading, the choice is not between good and evil; it is between good and good. Scepter and throne suggest authority and governance over others. While such power can certainly be abused, it is meant to be exercised in service. Of itself, it is good. Although wealth and prosperity can be acquired fraudulently, in the wisdom tradition they are usually regarded as rewards for righteous living. Even today health is considered a blessing from God, and beauty is always admired. The writer claims that, compared with wisdom, none of these has any value. Therefore, to choose any of them over wisdom is to choose emptiness. This is not far from Moses' admonition.

The man in the gospel does not ask merely for life; he asks for eternal life. He has been faithful, but he is not satisfied with having lived according to the commandments; he wants to do more. This is a good man: "Jesus, looking at him, loved him." In response to his own petition, Jesus admonishes him: "Go, sell what you have, and give to the poor." The man was startled. He could not accept the challenge. What Jesus asked was too much. The man was willing to do more, but he was unable to do with less.

Today we have two examples of how difficult choosing life can really be. The short reading from Hebrews underscores this. The word of God does indeed cut to the bone. It is incisive and probing. It leaves our inner being naked and exposed. However, each reading also includes a glimpse of the ultimate consequence of making the right choice. In the end, all the good things that were sacrificed in favor of wisdom came along with the possession of wisdom, and Jesus promised that those willing to forego earthly treasures will have treasure in heaven.

Is this a kind of Pollyanna pie-in-the-sky attempt to persuade us to choose the difficult path? Ask those who have made the choice. They tell us that despite what wealth and prosperity might afford, they do not guarantee fulfillment and happiness. We ourselves have often experienced a sense of well-being after having rendered service to others. Parents and friends are rewarded when they are able to help their loved ones to thrive. Teachers and health care personnel, engineers and carpenters give their time and talents freely to make life better for those who have little or nothing. They often enjoy personal satisfaction and the gratitude of those whom they have helped. In a very real way, they are blessed with a hundredfold of sisters and brothers whose lives they have touched.

Such unselfishness is real, but it is difficult. "For human beings it is impossible, but not for God." Jesus uses a graphic example to illustrate how hard it is for those who are encumbered to squeeze through a narrow opening. Nowhere in his teaching does he say that wealth is bad, but it can be a hindrance; it can get in the way if we selfishly hug it to ourselves.

Today's readings describe situations in which holding possessions is one of the options. But there are other "treasures" that we might be inclined to choose over wisdom or selflessness. Reputation is high on that list. How many people have not been tempted to fudge a bit in a business venture so that they might appear successful? What personal values are sometimes compromised for the sake of celebrity? What force might we be exerting against others in order to emerge as the undisputed "number one"? Personal comfort could also be the "camel" trying to squeeze through the eye of the needle. After all, why should we be the ones who are always called on to "go the extra mile"? Why should we have to worry about the children of someone else's war, or about the elderly poor who live their lives alone? If we are faithful to our obligations, if we have observed all of the commandments from our youth, shouldn't we be allowed to enjoy the fruits of our labor?

The readings challenge us today as they challenged others before us. I have set before you reputation and wisdom, comfort and eternal life. What will we choose?

Praying with Scripture

- Name two possessions that you most treasure. Do you use them wisely or selfishly?

- Is there anything in your life that prevents you from "passing through the eye of the needle"?

- Pray for the willingness to rid yourself of it, lest you overlook what is really necessary for your happiness.

TWENTY-NINTH SUNDAY IN ORDINARY TIME
Readings:
Isa 53:10–11; Ps 33:4–5, 18–20, 22;
Heb 4:14–16; Mark 10:35–45

WHAT'S THE POINT OF IT ALL?

Over the past few years, certain pictures have burned searing images into our memories. One is the published composite of hundreds of faces of rescue workers who never returned from the World Trade Center. Another is the row upon row of simple headstones on a well manicured bluff overlooking the tranquil beach of

Normandy. Many in our midst have not yet been released from images of the brutality endured in Southeast Asia. And these are only a few examples of the horrors that we carry around within us.

What is the point of all this suffering? If God is so good, why are we subjected to so much pain? People have always tried to provide answers to such questions. Many of these answers are found within our own religious tradition. Suffering is punishment for sin; it is a trial to test the mettle of our virtue; it is an opportunity to strengthen our inner being; or, as we find in the Book of Job, it is a mystery beyond our comprehension. I wonder whether the people referred to above would be satisfied with such answers.

The readings for today could be considered troublesome. The prophet Isaiah tells us that the servant was actually afflicted by God. The passage from Hebrews says that Christ too was tested. Then in the gospel, two of Jesus' closest companions are told that they must drink the cup of suffering that he drinks. These pictures do not offer a very consoling message. Was God really "pleased" to "crush" the servant of whom Isaiah spoke? Or did God allow the servant to be crushed so that others might somehow be saved? In the same vein, the author of Hebrews says that Christ, the great high priest, was tested so that we might receive mercy and find grace. In these readings, one person suffers for the sake of others. Is that fair? But is that the question placed before us today? Both the servant and Christ have moved beyond the question of whether or not suffering is fair, to the point where they seek to bring good out of suffering.

This still does not explain why there is suffering in the first place. Some have said that it exists because God has created an imperfect world. But is "imperfect" the right word to explain our world? Wouldn't it be better to say that God created a world that is in constant flux? Every branch of science today recognizes this flux without labeling it "imperfect." The pains of growth and diminishment are part of that flux, as is some of the suffering born of some human choices. Does that make the world imperfect?

On the other hand, we cannot deny that sometimes we make deliberate sinful decisions, and these decisions do in fact spawn suffering in ourselves and in others. But to acknowledge this is quite different from claiming that suffering is a punishment from God.

Once again we are thrown back onto the incomprehensibility of this mystery. We do not always understand why there is suffering.

The message of these first two readings has little or nothing to do with the "why" of suffering. Rather, the readings focus on the value that might be derived from it. This theme is developed in the gospel. The brothers James and John realize how privileged they are to be numbered among Jesus' closest friends, and they seek the glory that they presume accompanies such privilege. Much to their surprise, Jesus offers them a share in his own cup of suffering. They are told that the way to exercise authority over others is through service for them. Jesus' words should alert us to the reversal of perspective that following him so often requires. If discipleship and leadership are to be understood in a new way, perhaps the same is true for suffering.

Phrases such as "offering for sin," "tested in every way," "give [one's] life as a ransom for many" are not the kind of theological language that we normally use today. However, we do understand unselfish service, the willingness to risk one's life for another, and commitment to others beyond the call of duty. In such circumstances, a heavy price is often exacted, even though we might not give a second thought to the suffering involved.

Suffering of various kinds and intensities explodes in the life of every human being. We cannot stave it off, regardless of how innocent we may be. If we are to be true followers of Christ, we will have to learn how we might use the vicissitudes of life to accomplish something good. When we make this decision, we might find ourselves saying: "Take my arm; lean on me; let me help." Or: "I will not retaliate; I will not seek revenge; the anger and violence will stop with me." Or: "I will do whatever I can so that no one else will have to endure what I have endured." The grace of God helps us to see that there can be a point to suffering.

Praying with Scripture

- Be grateful for the many ways that you have been blessed through someone else's hardships borne on your behalf.

- In what ways might your own suffering be of benefit to others?

- Pray for patience and courage as you endure the suffering in your life.

THIRTIETH SUNDAY IN ORDINARY TIME

Readings:
Jer 31:7–9; Ps 126:1–6;
Heb 5:1–6; Mark 10:46–52

WHAT DID YOU EXPECT?

Several years ago Bishop Kenneth Untener, the bishop of Saginaw, Michigan, reminded a seminary graduating class that building ramps will not give the disabled back the use of their legs. In other words, ministry does not always turn circumstances around. Sometimes the most it can do is hold back the tide of misfortune, or provide a raft so people are not swallowed up by dangerous currents. In other words, ramps simply make it easier for those who are disabled to enter a building.

After we build ramps, however, or set aside parking places, or provide aids for hearing and seeing, we sometimes conclude that we have done our part, and it's now time to move on to the next project. We might look upon those whose needs cannot be easily remedied in the same way the disciples in the gospel looked upon the beggar who was blind. To them he was an annoyance, not because of his blindness but because they were leaving Jericho heading to Jerusalem and he was disrupting their plans.

The readings today deal with the reign of God. At first glance, they look like success stories, because in them circumstances have been turned around. The blind man receives his sight. In Jeremiah's future, those who are blind or lame or with children or who are pregnant are gathered together again. And the picture of Christ the high priest is truly glorious. A closer look reveals something different. Jeremiah's scene depicts the people who had been scattered by the exile, people who were afflicted and especially vulnerable. They were gathered together and consoled and cared for by God, but the text does not say that they were healed. Hebrews does depict Christ the high priest, but it indicates that he was glorified only after he had sacrificed himself for the sake of others. It was the blind man's own faith that saved him. New Testament scholars tell us that *this* was the true miracle. His healing was simply the external manifestation of his faith.

These are truly success stories, but not in ways that we might at first have thought. The successes that they depict can be seen in God's embrace of those who have been broken by life's tragedies, in Jesus' total giving of himself for others, and in the faith of the man who called upon Jesus. In each instance, something of the reign of God was brought to light. This reign exists underneath, behind, or deep within the circumstances of life, even if we cannot see it there. It takes shape when we embrace the needy in our midst, when we give of ourselves to others, when we turn to Jesus in faith. Bringing this reign to light is the responsibility of us all, not merely of those for whom it is a professional responsibility. Baptism has made us all ministers of this reign, and our place in the world, as circumscribed as that might be, is our field of ministry.

The reign of God does not always meet our expectations. It would be wonderful if those who are blind or lame would be healed through faith, but they are not. It would be wonderful if those who are in any way vulnerable would be strengthened and preserved from harm, but that does not happen either. Hence, there will always be people who need our help, and in helping them we will establish the reign of God. It is almost as if we need them so that we can bring God's reign to our world. Perhaps we do need them! We always say that the reign of God turns circumstances upside down. Might this turn of events be an example of such a reversal? Perhaps it is our turn to cry out: "Master, I want to see."

Other expectations surrounding the reign of God have been dashed as well. Those committed to ministry have not always been faithful to their charge. The disciples were not always good ministers. They tried to silence the man. Some who minister have been guilty of greed, blind ambition, or the abuse of power. Why did God choose weak human beings to establish that reign on earth? How can a reign of holiness be brought forth by sinners?

Those committed to ministry are also often disappointed. They do not always see their work bear the fruit they had hoped it would. At times their best intentions are questioned, and their commitment is dismissed by the very ones they serve. This is particularly true when people of genuine integrity and unselfishness are forced to bear the shame and suspicion brought on by the crimes of others. The establishment of the reign of God does not appear to be a success story in our day.

But maybe it is. Are there not among us those who embrace the needy? Are there not among us those willing to sacrifice themselves for others? Perhaps if we have faith, our eyes will be opened and we will see how the reign of God is indeed being established in our midst.

Praying with Scripture

- How is the reign of God taking shape in the world in which you live?

- How do you contribute to the establishment of this reign?

- Make a point to thank those in your acquaintance who are faithful ministers.

THIRTY-FIRST SUNDAY IN ORDINARY TIME
Readings:
Deut 6:2–6; Ps 18:2–4, 47, 51;
Heb 7:23–28; Mark 12:28b–34

"TAKE TO HEART THESE WORDS"

Some Christians have erroneously accused the Old Testament of being legalistic. This most likely comes from a misunderstanding of Paul's insistence that faith in Christ, not obser-

vance of the law, is what saves. Paul never really condemned
Jewish law; he obeyed it. What he rejected was any thought that
we might earn salvation by observing the law. It is true that large
sections of Exodus, Leviticus, Numbers, and Deuteronomy contain collections of both social and religious legislation. However,
these laws developed over many centuries and were finally gathered in one place in the Bible. Most of the Old Testament is nar-
rative or poetry, not law. Were we to gather all the laws legislated
in our country within the last year, we would realize how small
the corpus of biblical law really is.

Old Testament law can be accurately understood only within
the context of covenant. While God initiated the covenant, the
Israelites understood it in terms of ancient legal treaties between
gods and their devotees. One of the features of a particular
covenant formula is a statement by the deity of all the blessings
bestowed on the people. This is followed by a list of the reciprocal
responsibilities of the covenant partners. It is as if the god were
saying: "If you want to be in covenant with me, this is the way you
should live." Israel's law fits into this kind of covenant relationship
with God. Some of its laws describe the way the people should pay
homage to God. Since all covenants have a social dimension, however, the law also includes responsibilities toward others.

The reading from Deuteronomy contains what many con-
sider to be the most significant prayer of the Israelite religion. It is
a prayer still recited by observant Jews, and it frequently became
the last words of testimony on the lips of persecuted Jews: "Hear,
O Israel! The LORD is our God, the LORD alone!" This profession
of faith is found within a summons to obedience: "Hear…and be
careful to observe…." It is followed by the well-known directive:
"You shall love the LORD, your God, with all your heart, and with
all your soul, and with all your strength." While the Hebrew word
love does at times include some degree of emotional attachment, its
primary focus is fidelity to commitment. In this passage it means
that the covenant partner must be committed to God completely.
Simple external conformity to law is not enough. All interior fac-
ulties are to be involved in this commitment. This includes the
heart, which was considered the seat of mind and will; the soul,
which was thought to be the source of vitality; and all of one's
strength. The passage ends with the injunction: "Take to heart

these words which I enjoin on you today." In other words, commit your entire self to God, and take this commitment seriously.

In the gospel, the man who posed the question to Jesus was not ignorant of the law. He was a scribe, schooled in the intricacies of the law. Jesus' comment at the end of the story suggests that this was a genuine question seeking clarification. If he was an expert, why did he need clarification? By the time of Jesus, the law had developed into 613 precepts. Though all of them were binding, some were regarded as "heavy" or very important and others were looked upon as "less weighty." The scribe asked Jesus which one of these precepts was the greatest. Jesus linked two of them that are not identical, but they are interrelated: Love God; and love your neighbor. The expression used by Jesus was taken right out of the covenant theology of Deuteronomy. It crystallizes into two injunctions all the law found in the tradition. Jesus might well have ended his answer with a quote from the great Jewish scholar Hillel: "All the rest is commentary."

The scribe asked for one commandment, and Jesus gave him two. Just what is the relationship between these two? There are two ways of looking at this relationship. The first develops out of the theology of covenant; the second from the notion of body of Christ. The covenant reflected in today's reading was made between God and Israel as an entire people. It resulted in a definite social bonding as well. Therefore, the Israelites' love of (commitment to) God was demonstrated in the way they interacted with God's other covenant partners, and their love of these other partners demonstrated the character of their love of God. "Body of Christ" theology is much more explicit. As members of Christ we are joined to each other. This union is clearly stated in another gospel: "Whatever you did for one of these…you did for me" (Matt 25:40).

When we love another completely, we also love those who are loved by that person. So it is with the love of God. When we love God completely, we also love those whom God loves. And in loving others, we are doing what God does.

Praying with Scripture

- How, other than through prescribed religious observance, do you demonstrate your love for God?

- Perform one or two explicit acts of kindness this week.

- Spend some time reflecting on the responsorial psalm.

THIRTY-SECOND SUNDAY IN ORDINARY TIME
Readings:
1 Kgs 17:10–16; Ps 146:7, 8–10;
Heb 9:24–28; Mark 12:38–44

GIVING UNTIL IT HURTS

Very few of us give until it hurts. Actually, for some people it hurts just to give. Then when we do give, we often expect a reciprocal gift in return; or we claim a tax deduction for our trouble; or a plaque is set up in remembrance of our generosity, or, if we have given a large sum of money, we might even have a building named after us. We do not always give unselfishly, as did the two women we read about today.

It is significant that these two women were widows. This does not simply mean that their husbands had died. It means that, with no male patron, they had no place in the patriarchal structure of society. There was no one to ensure their rights and provide for their welfare. Most widows did not return to the homes of their fathers, nor did they always find refuge with their brothers. The first widow was still caring for her son, and so there was no assistance from him. No family members are mentioned in the gospel account. Widows with no family support were one of the most vulnerable groups in that patriarchal society. Yet these are the ones who gave until it hurt.

The desperate plight of the first widow is drawn with bold strokes. As a widow, she not only lives on the margins of society, but she is also destitute and on the brink of starvation. To make matters worse, she has a child who is in the same straits. It is to this woman that the prophet turns. At first she hesitates, but when he promises that God will provide for her and her son, she acquiesces to his request. She places her trust in the words of the prophet, and they are fulfilled. The woman in the gospel reading did not know that she was being observed. Unlike some in the crowd who make a show of their temple offering, she chose to be inconspicuous. Her offering was meager compared to others, but it had great significance. She gave out of generosity, not out of any abundance. Both of these women already hurt, and yet they gave more.

The lessons in these stories are obvious. The first is a clear willingness to give, regardless of how small the gift might be. The giving depicted here springs from generosity of heart, not simply financial advantage. A second lesson is religious devotion. The widow of Zarephath was a woman of faith. She trusted in the words of the prophet. The woman who came to the temple was also a woman of faith. She sought to do her part in temple support. The third lesson is care of others. Despite her own wretched situation, the first woman cared not only for her son who depended upon her, but also for the prophet for whom she had no personal responsibility. In the second instance, some of the temple donations went for the support of temple personnel. These women show that in genuine giving you do not always have the opportunity to decide how your money will be used. One simply gives where there is need.

There are many ways that we can all "give until it hurts." Monetary giving is only one of them. We can first give our care and interest. This is not as easy as it sounds, particularly in societies that value personal advancement and satisfaction above all else, that dismiss the concerns of others as unimportant or boring compared to one's own, that promote suspicion of religious or ethnic bigotry, that tolerate violence and war. Despite the obstacles we might encounter, we can share our talents with others in our families, our neighborhoods, and our parish churches. We can give our time and our energy in schools, in hospitals, and in soup kitchens. Sometimes it is much easier to give money than to give ourselves in ways such as these.

There are many people in our world, however, who are generous as these widows were. Like the woman from Zarephath, they are committed to the well-being of their children. Many parents willingly sacrifice their own interests so that their children have what they need and some of what they want. There are people who work long hours in health-care facilities, making sure that the needs of patients and residents are being met. Public servants such as police and firefighters place themselves at risk in order to ensure our safety. We find notable unselfishness in those who serve in the military. Those who minister in the church often do so at great financial expense and sometimes with little hope of appreciation from those whom they serve.

The ultimate example of unselfish giving is Jesus, who is characterized in today's second reading as the perfect victim offered to God for our sakes. He gave until he had no more to give. He sacrificed his own interests for our good; he devoted himself to our healing; he gave his life that we might live; and he did all this with little hope of appreciation.

Praying with Scripture

- Who are the people in your life who have given to you until it hurts? If you have the opportunity, thank them.

- In what ways have you held back when asked to give? Pray for the strength and courage to do better.

- Do something concrete for someone who is less fortunate than you.

THIRTY-THIRD SUNDAY IN ORDINARY TIME
Readings:
Dan 12:1–3; Ps 16:5, 8–11;
Heb 10:11–14, 18; Mark 13:24–32

TRADITIONAL "NEW AGE" THEOLOGY

Both the first and the third readings for today begin with the words "In those days." Of which days are the writers speaking?

And why are they so filled with terror and destruction? These accounts reflect ancient Israelite understanding of the end time (a time of fulfillment not to be confused with the end of time). Israel believed that the sinful age within which it was living would come to an end and an age of holiness would follow. However, the period of transition from one age to the other would be a time of purification. Initially, Israel expected this to transpire in history. This is why the end time was different from the end of time.

There were various traditions regarding the way this new age would dawn. Some believed that a descendant of David would establish a new and faithful rule (Acts 1:6). Others, like the Qumran community that settled near the Dead Sea, expected a priestly leader to launch a cultic reform. Still others looked for someone from heaven to inaugurate the new age. In line with this last tradition, Jesus describes "the Son of Man coming in the clouds." Of which days do today's authors speak? Clearly the time of transition between the ages. Why are "those days" filled with terror? It is because they include purification from sin. When will they dawn? That is the sixty-four thousand dollar question!

The reading from Daniel suggests that "those days" refers to the end time. Scholars question whether the author is really referring to resurrection of the dead or to what some call "the rapture" ("your people shall escape"). Instead, they remind us that Daniel was written in a kind of code called apocalyptic, which prevented Israel's conquerors from detecting the book's subversive message. In other words, it means what it says, but on a level that is not always obvious. Its promise of future justice encouraged the beleaguered people to remain faithful in the face of affliction. The reading from Mark is also apocalyptic. Though it suggests the end of the world ("Heaven and earth will pass away"), scholars believe that it refers primarily to the destruction of Jerusalem. As with the first reading, it encouraged fidelity at a time when their world seemed to be falling apart. This reading clearly states that no one but God knows when the end will come.

Though both readings describe frightful scenes, they also assert that the righteous will somehow survive the ordeal and will find a place with God. This hopeful message continues to console those who are forced to watch their own worlds fall apart. Both Daniel and Mark offer resounding negative responses to gnawing questions such as: "Does our suffering mean that evil forces have the last word? Has God forgotten us? Have the righteous dead died in vain?"

Why are these readings placed before us now? They certainly are relevant. Who has not struggled with, and sometimes been overcome by, the evil forces let loose in our world today? Who has not asked the questions posed above? We desperately need both the comfort and the encouragement that these readings offer, even though we may have to look beneath the scenes that they sketch to find their real meaning. On one level they may indeed speak of the actual end of the world when Christ will come "'in the clouds' with great power and glory." However, it is not only then that we will move from one age to another. Christians believe that the new age has already been inaugurated with the coming of Jesus into history. That is why we have these readings at the end of the liturgical year as we turn our gaze toward the celebration of that coming.

Our understanding of the end time has yet a third level. Though the new age dawned with Jesus' coming, it only takes root in us when we open ourselves to its power. Each time we are willing to move beyond our sinfulness, despite the "distress" or "tribulation" this may cause, we step over the threshold into the new age. The two transitions from old to new described in the readings are beyond our control, but the transition of personal transformation is ours to make. Our decision to bring the new age to light in a way puts an end to part of the world of sin. To use another image, the struggle to bring the reign of God to birth has been called the "labor pains" of the Messiah (Matt 24:8; Rom 8:22). Such pain can be life-giving.

As we approach the end of the liturgical year, our religious perspective focuses on the coming of the Lord. But which coming? His first coming according to the flesh when he inaugurated the end time? His final coming that we expect at the end of time? Or his coming into our lives each time we step forward in genuine Christian living? Actually, all three comings have immense meaning for our lives.

Praying with Scripture

- What about the end of the world do you fear? Why?

- Why do you look forward to the celebration of Jesus' coming in human flesh?

- Might God be calling you to leave the old age for the new one?

CHRIST THE KING
Readings:
Dan 7:13–14; Ps 93:1–2, 5;
Rev 1:5–8; John 18:33b–37

WHAT A VISION!

Kingship is not very popular today. For that matter, nor is queenship. In a world in which most people favor democratic governance, rule by one person can seem to be too close to tyranny for comfort. But such rule is not really what today's feast is about. The gospel tells us that Jesus himself rejected the notion of human kingship. Then what are we commemorating?

The readings describe enthronement in heaven. Daniel tells of the mysterious Son of Man, with whom Jesus would later identify himself, coming on the clouds, glorified by God and given dominion that will last forever. In the reading from Revelation, the Risen Christ comes amid the clouds as the Alpha and the Omega, the first and the last of all things. These cosmic images have very little to do with royal rule as we know it.

Christ's enthronement in heaven recalls elements of an ancient Near Eastern myth of creation. In it, after the cosmic warrior-god defeated the monster of chaos and established order in the universe, this god was enthroned in a palace constructed for him in the heavens. From this throne he ruled over all creation. Ancient Israel reshaped this myth, casting its own God in the role of vic-

torious king. This is the background of today's psalm that praises
the majesty of the creator-god. Finally, as they did with so much
of ancient Israelite tradition, New Testament writers reinter-
preted the story from a Christian point of view. While the Christian
reinterpretation of this cosmic drama shares many of the characteristics of the other versions, it highlights significant differences.
First, Christ certainly did overcome the powers of evil and chaos.
He did it, not through force of arms, but by emptying himself of
all divine privilege (Phil 2:6–7) and enduring bitter suffering and
an ignominious death. He is indeed enthroned over all. However,
he won this distinction, not through the conquest of another, but
through the shedding of his own blood.

It is of this rule that Jesus speaks in the gospel when he
asserts that his kingdom "does not belong to this world." He emptied kingship of its conventional significance and gave his reign a
new meaning. He rules through service of others, rather than
through domination of them. His authority is rooted in truth, not
physical force. When Jesus said that his kingdom was "not of this
world," he did not mean that it was not *in* this world. He constantly called people to live lives of justice and compassion,
understanding and generosity. His kingdom, the reign of God, is
based on the Beatitudes, not on some of the principles that seem
to have such a hold on modern society.

Apocalyptic is an apt way of describing the "otherworldli-
ness" of Jesus' rule. While its exotic character seems to carry us
out of space and time, it really invites us into a deeper dimension
of reality, one beneath the surface. Apocalyptic may include
descriptions of frightful disasters, but these disasters are always
resolved, and good triumphs over evil—just as we saw in the
ancient story of the primeval victory over chaos. In other words,
the apocalyptic message is one of hope.

These apocalyptic readings have meaning for the feast of
Christ the King, for the end of the liturgical year, and for the
world in which we find ourselves today. First, they remind us of
the nature of the authentic rule of Christ. It is a rule of victory
through self-giving. It is a rule where authority springs from
truth. Whenever we follow the example set for us by Christ, we
participate *in* this world, in the reign of God that is *not of* this
world. The liturgical year is a kind of journey through the mys-

teries of salvation. The end of the year, which we mark today, brings us to the end of the journey, and here we find the victorious Christ enthroned in glory. In faith we believe that he has indeed conquered the forces of sin and death, and he is already enthroned with God. In anticipation, we look forward to his final glorious appearance.

How is this theology relevant today? So much in this world could lead to hopelessness. Besides the usual pitfalls that we always find on the path of life, today we have come to realize that in no place on the globe are we really safe. Furthermore, our confidence in both religious and political leadership has been shaken. Finally, job security has collapsed; poverty has eaten away the fabric of many communities; and crime seems to be rampant. For many, circumstances appear to be going from bad to worse. This feast with its apocalyptic themes could not have come at a better time. They remind us that the battle has already been won; Christ is really triumphant. Now it is up to us to make his reign present in our world.

Praying with Scripture

- What person's life models for you Jesus' self-emptying love?

- What keeps you from living under the rule of Jesus the Christ?

- Precisely what might you do to further God's reign on earth?

Solemnities and Feasts

TRINITY SUNDAY (SOLEMNITY)

Readings:

Deut 4:32–34, 39–40; Ps 33:4–6, 9, 18–20, 22;
Rom 8:14–17; Matt 28:16–20

WHO IS GOD?

Who is God? God is "the infinite divine being, one in being yet three Persons." This is the definition given in the Catechism, where we find direct questions and concise answers. It is all so clear on paper, but it sounds so impersonal. At least the question "who?" suggests that God is personal and not an impersonal "what." The Catechism may offer an accurate theological answer, but it in no way explains how the doctrine of the Trinity, which is the central tenet of our faith, really touches our lives. However, the readings for today's feast provide us with glimpses into this mystery, fleeting as these glimpses might be. They create a kind of collage that leaves us with impressions, but still not a clear picture. But then how can we hope to grasp even a corner of the mystery that is behind everything that exists?

The first reading takes us back into the wilderness with the newly delivered Israelite people. In order to impress on these people the importance of a particular way of life, Moses reminds them of the extraordinary character of the God who calls for such a commitment. This is not a deity who simply seeks to control lives; this God is the source of life itself. This is a God who took personal interest in a relatively insignificant people, leading them out of Egyptian bondage amid signs and wonders, miraculously caring for them in the stark wilderness, and finally going ahead of them into a land within which they would settle and eventually thrive.

This same God continues to show interest in us today. To use the words of the great Jewish philosopher Martin Buber: This is a God who is not only *with* us, but who is *for* us as well. To be *for* us means that God has our best interests in mind. This glimpse into God's concern for us is at odds with the contemporary claim that the apparent randomness of the forces of nature invalidates the notion of a personal God. In this regard, science does not contradict faith. Rather, it calls us to look at faith in a new way. The very consistency in the physical activity of the universe suggests that there is a power upon which we can rely and in which we can trust. In other words, it is not only with us, but it has our best interests in mind. Believers maintain that this power is divine.

In his Letter to the Romans, Paul makes an astonishingly bold statement, telling us that we have "received a Spirit of adoption, through whom we cry, 'Abba, Father!'" We are not only a chosen people, "we are children of God." The ancients characterized some of their gods as fathers, because they considered human fathers the source of life, loving protectors, and attentive guides. In those patriarchal societies, only a male child could be an heir. This explains the importance given to sons. Today we are aware of the gender biases present in these characterizations. However, the relational attributes underlying these characterizations continue to point to profoundly intimate bonds. When Paul declares that we are heirs of God, "joint heirs with Christ," he is saying that we enjoy a relationship that is both with God as Father and with Christ who is now our brother. These relationships are anything but impersonal. They lift us up into the very life of God.

What we know about the divine nature, we know from Jesus. He told us that he proceeded from the Father and that the Spirit is his own Spirit. It is through Jesus that we were brought into the intimacy of the divine "family," baptized into its threefold name: "...in the name of the Father, and of the Son, and of the Holy Spirit." Jesus' life, death, and resurrection shout to the heavens the extent to which "God so loved the world" (John 3:16). There is no concrete evidence that can legitimate these claims. Like the disciples before us, all we can do is accept them in faith.

We may not be able to grasp the character of the Trinity in itself, but if we do accept these claims, we come to realize who God is for us. We know from Jesus, and from our own experience, that God is indeed with us and for us. We know that God creates, because we are immersed in the wonders of the created world; we are in fact a marvelous example of God's creative artistry. We know that God sustains creation, because we are cared for by the very world within which we live. It provides us with the nourishment and warmth that we need to survive, as well as with the natural beauty that sustains our spirits. We know that God saves, because even now we are being freed from the bondage of our addictions, from the tyranny of our demons, from the hatred and greed that can consume us. Whether or not we understand the Catechism's answers, today's readings assure us that we live in the embrace of the loving triune God.

Praying with Scripture

- Reflect on times when you experienced that God was *with* you.

- In what ways have you come to realize that God is for you, wanting what is in your best interest?

- Spend time today reflecting on what it means to be a child of God.

MOST HOLY BODY AND BLOOD OF CHRIST (SOLEMNITY)

Readings:
Exod 24:3–8; Ps 116:12–13, 15–18; Heb 9:11–15; Mark 14:12–16, 22–26

THE MERCIES OF THE LORD ARE NEW EVERY MORNING!

What were once two feasts, namely, Corpus Christi and Precious Blood, are now one celebration. Originally the first feast honored the body of Christ that was first broken, then glorified, and is now given to us in sacramental form. The second feast honored the blood of Christ, which was poured out on the cross for our salvation. Together, the two feasts commemorate the incomparable love that Christ has for us. The gospel reading opens with a reference to "the first day of the Feast of Unleavened Bread, when they sacrificed the Passover lamb." Thus we see that two religious feasts were also combined at the time of Jesus. The feast of Unleavened Bread was observed with bread that lacked any trace of fermenting yeast. This prescription reminded the people of the time of the first Passover, when they left Egypt before their bread had time to rise. The feast of Passover itself was the commemoration of their deliverance from Egyptian bondage. They were saved if their homes were marked with the blood of the sacrificed lamb.

Breaking bread, or eating, with other people is a very familiar human act. Besides being a basic act of human survival, it signifies that we are sharing with others the very means of our common sustenance. There is a basic twofold meaning here. First, we eat the same food, because we are all made of the same substance. Second, we eat with others because this simple yet profound communal act binds us to them at the very core of our being, that is, physical survival. Finally, eating together demonstrates a certain degree of trust, because when we eat we lower our guard somewhat, thus leaving ourselves vulnerable to the other.

When Jesus took bread, blessed it, broke it, and gave it to his disciples to eat, he was enacting this fundamental ritual, namely, people surviving together on the same food. Though he must have performed this ritual on numerous occasions, for it was a very common Jewish practice, it took on extraordinary meaning when he did it at what was to be his last supper. The ritual of blessing, breaking, and sharing bread was the same as other rituals before it; the original meaning was not lost. It was the character of the bread that made the difference this time. By Jesus' own words, this broken bread was now his own body that would be broken and then raised to glory. Now this simple yet profound action signified that those at table were bound to him and to one another in a new way.

Contemporary society holds at least two attitudes toward the use of blood. The role that it plays in the ritual described in today's first reading probably repels most modern people. After sacrificing the requisite number of animals, Moses splashed some of their blood on the altar and other blood on the people gathered around it. If we sometimes shield ourselves from the ritual sprinkling of holy water, we will hardly appreciate being sprinkled with blood. On the other hand, blood is recognized as a life force, and so generally we value blood transfusions and the possibilities envisioned by the use of blood in stem cell research. Furthermore, blood relationships are some of the most cherished bonds that we know, and they have both social and legal ramifications that are quite binding. Thus blood and blood bonds continue to play important roles in our lives today.

The readings for this feast are rich with profound theological themes and moving religious sentiment. In the first reading we see God making a binding pact with the Israelites and sealing this pact with blood. The use of blood underscores the seriousness of the bond. Blood also reminded the covenant partners of the possible penalty of violation of the covenant agreement. We then stand speechless before the reading from the Letter to the Hebrews. There we discover that the blood that sealed our fate as Christians is actually the blood of Jesus. This reading focuses on a different sacrificial offering, one in which blood is offered in reparation for sin. In ancient Israel, the ritual of sprinkling over the "mercy seat," which covered the Ark of the Covenant, was performed once a year. The Christian writer insists that Jesus' offering was once for all and would not have to be offered again. Finally, the gospel passage is a report of the first eucharistic meal. Knowing that soon he would be facing his own death, Jesus' thoughts were with his disciples. He invited them, and us with them, to renew the eternal covenant pact made with us all each time we partake of the blood of the covenant. As we take the broken bread that has been transformed into Jesus' own body and drink from the cup of his blood that he offers us, we realize that indeed the mercies of the Lord are new every morning.

Praying with Scripture

- Spend a few moments prayerfully reading the Sequence for the Solemnity of the Most Holy Body and Blood of Christ: "Laud, O Zion, your salvation."

- On the occasion of this feast, recommit yourself to the covenant sealed by the blood of Christ.

- Reflect on the importance of the Eucharist in your life.

PRESENTATION OF THE LORD (FEAST)
Readings:
Mal 3:1–4; Ps 24:7–10;
Heb 2:14–18; Luke 2:22–40

LIFT UP, O GATES, YOUR LINTELS!

There was a time when the parish church was the center of activity. Not only did parishioners go there for worship and participation in religious devotions, but it also offered a sense of community. If the parish had no school, it offered catechism classes for children of all ages. Men were members of the Holy Name Society, and women belonged to the Christian Mothers. There were dances and picnics, rummage sales and raffles. Everyone knew everyone else, because the parish was in one's neighborhood, and the other parishioners were family members and neighbors.

This is generally no longer the case. Society is much more complex, and this has altered the character of the parish community in significant ways. Other organizations provide for social involvement. Dances are held in clubs around the city. Raffles have been replaced by the lottery, which does not require one's presence. If there are parish boundaries, they are ignored and people attend liturgy wherever they feel comfortable. They no longer worship with their neighbors, and they may not even know the people with whom they do worship. All of this has contributed to the difficulty parish ministers face as they attempt to create a sense of community among their parishioners.

There are reasons why the church was the center of parish life. In this country, its early immigrant character played a significant role. For the newly arrived and their descendants, the church and all that it offered were vestiges of home. It was a place where their language of origin was respected and spoken, where ethnic customs were preserved and concerns regarding acculturation shared. This may still be the case for the new immigrants.

The social function of the church notwithstanding, the primary reason that it was the center of Christian life was the belief that it was there we met God. This concept was reinforced by the sacramental presence of the Lord in the Eucharist. Before the Second Vatican Council broadened our perspective to appreciate the presence of Christ in the Christian community itself, the church was considered the home of God on earth. An idea similar to this was cherished by the Jewish community, as we see in the readings for today's feast.

The temple was prized as the place where God was present among the people. They believed that it was built on the *axis mundi*, or the center of the world. This *axis* was considered the most important spot on Earth, for it was the point where heaven, Earth, and the underworld met. Because of this location and its role as God's dwelling place on Earth, the temple was accorded cosmic significance. This explains why sacrifices were offered there and major feasts celebrated. A visit to the temple was considered a religious event. People hoped that there they would experience something of God.

The responsorial psalm for today was probably part of the celebration of a religious pilgrimage. It suggests that God is leading the people to the temple. As they approached its walls, they would cry out: "Lift up, O gates, your lintels... / that the king of glory may come in," to which the temple personnel would reply: "Who is this king of glory?" In response to this question, they would identify God as the divine warrior, the great creator-god who conquered the primordial forces of chaos. The cosmic character of the temple, mentioned above, is behind the imagery of the psalm.

The reading from the prophet Malachi originated at a time when the holiness of the temple had been marred by the sinfulness of its personnel (the sons of Levi). The fierceness of the purification they would face is startling. The holiness that the people ascribed to the temple, however, required complete purification. The prophet announces that the Lord is indeed coming to the temple, but to bring punishment, not blessing.

The gospel recounts the event of Jesus' presentation in the temple. It actually mentions two religious rituals. The first is the purification of Mary, which the law prescribed after a woman gave birth (Lev 12:1–5). After a specific period of time, she was required to present herself at the temple to be reinstated into full participation in the community. The real focus of the reading is on the second ritual, the redemption of the first-born, a tradition that was traced back to the time of the exodus from Egypt (Exod 13:2, 12). The significance of Jesus' coming to the temple for this ritual was recognized by Simeon and Anna, devout people who spent time there in prayer. They knew that they had encountered the promised one of God, and they believed that their expectations were now fulfilled.

Our parish churches may no longer be the center of our lives, as they were in the past. But where do we encounter God today? Vatican II helped us see that Christ is present in the community, especially when it gathers to worship. But is that our experience? If not, are we doing anything to remedy it?

Praying with Scripture

- Where do you go to reflect on and experience the presence of God in your life?

- How faithful are you in observing and celebrating religious practices?

- In what ways might you contribute to the community life of your parish?

NATIVITY OF ST. JOHN THE BAPTIST (SOLEMNITY)

Readings:
Isa 49:1–6; Ps 139:1–3, 13–15;
Acts 13:22–26; Luke 1:57–66, 80

"BEHOLD, ONE IS COMING AFTER ME"

Several paradoxes surround the figure of John the Baptist. He is said to have been a relative of Jesus, and yet one does not get the impression from the gospels that they knew each other very well. His father was a priest, but he did not conform to the prevailing custom of following in his father's footsteps. He recognized Jesus while they were both in the womb (Luke 1:41), and he identified him as the "Lamb of God" to some of his own followers (John 1:29). Yet at one point he seems to have had some doubts about Jesus' ministry (Matt 11:3). Jesus extols John with the words: "Among those born of women there has been none greater than John the Baptist"; then he reduces his status: "Yet the least in the kingdom of heaven is greater than he" (Matt 11:11). Finally, though he was never a follower of Jesus, his birthday is marked on the Christian calendar.

Like the feast of the nativity of Jesus, that of John the Baptist falls on one of the solstices, a hinge point in the cosmos. These were times of seasonal change, of cosmic reversal. They were times when the entire universe was being alerted, and something new was about to happen. Some early Christian writings saw great significance in this. According to them, the birth of Jesus was placed in the calendar when, in the northern hemisphere, the days begin to lengthen and the sun begins to appear again in all of its brilliance. The date of John's birthday was so chosen precisely because the days were getting shorter. In this way, the calendar actually demonstrates the truth of John's declaration: "He must increase; I must decrease" (John 3:30).

John is also a hinge between the old age and the new. He was the herald, the one who announced Jesus' coming. However, he never took the step into the time of fulfillment that Jesus brought to birth. He lived a life of great austerity and he preached repentance, neither of which is particularly inviting. Still, he attracted crowds of people from every walk of life. They left the comfort of the cities to listen to him in the wilderness and to be baptized in the Jordan River. Many of the people must have thought that he himself was the promised one of God, because he had to assure them that he was not and that the one coming after him was much greater than he. In fact, he was not even worthy to provide him the meanest service. This is the man whose birthday we celebrate today.

So many of the details of John's birth are extraordinary. First, he was born of a woman who was considered too old to have conceived. Second, his birth was announced to his father by an angel. Then, because the father did not believe the angel's words, he was rendered speechless. This condition lasted until the child was born and his father insisted that he be given the name indicated by the angel. The name, which means "God is gracious," could refer to God's goodness in granting the couple a child. Or it could refer to the astonishing plan of salvation within which the child would eventually play a pivotal role. The author of the Acts of the Apostles provides a sketch of this plan and describes the role that he played in it.

Though the reading from Israel, referred to as one of the "servant songs," has never been considered a tradition theologically linked with John, details surrounding his birth are reminiscent of the description found in these verses: called from birth; named while in his mother's womb; honed like a sharp-edged sword. If not *the* "servant of the Lord," John was certainly *a* servant, called to announce the good news of God's salvation.

It is no wonder that people flocked to John. He was a remarkable man, true to his destiny, never wavering to the left or to the right. As early as the time of his naming, the neighbors recognized this: "What, then, will this child be?" They realized that "the hand of the Lord was with him." Their evaluation of him corresponded with Jesus' description given many years later. John was truly one called by God and sent to prepare the way of the Lord.

It is not enough to marvel at this exceptional man. He has lessons to teach us. Through baptism we have all been called by

God, and we all play a role in God's plan of salvation. We may not know precisely what it is, but it will come clear in time. Most of us will not be expected to live austere lives as John did, but we all have the responsibility of dedicating ourselves to God and preparing the way of the Lord. Like John we must grow and become strong in spirit. Regardless of our place in the world, we can all point to the Lord by the way we live.

Praying with Scripture

- Do you recognize the promptings of God in your life? Or do you doubt God's power to accomplish what is astonishing, as John's father did?

- Reflect on your life. In what ways does it demonstrate that you are a disciple of Jesus?

- Are you able to step back and allow others to take your work in another direction? Pray to John the Baptist for that grace.

SAINTS PETER AND PAUL (SOLEMNITY)
Readings:
Acts 12:1–11; Ps 34:2–9;
2 Tim 4:6–8, 17–18; Matt 16:13–19

THE WEAK OF THE WORLD

We might be somewhat intimidated when we read the lives of saints such as the two men whose feast we celebrate today. Saints are often depicted as people who are bigger than life. Their courage and commitment to God are placed before us as models to emulate. This is all fine, as long as we remember that they were flesh and blood people, probably no different than we are, at least at some time in their lives. What made them extraordinary was the grace of God that worked through them. Before their days were devoted to ministry to and within the young church, both Peter and Paul had very ordinary occupations. Peter was a fisherman, and Paul a tentmaker. But once they became aware of who Jesus really was, their entire lives were reoriented, and the spread of the gospel became their preoccupation.

The weaknesses of both Peter and Paul are well known to all. However, we sometimes seem to take them lightly, even find them rather humorous. We use the expression "knocked off your high horse," a reference to the dramatic event of Paul's conversion, to describe putting someone in his or her place. As clever as it might sound, it is an incorrect caricature of what happened, and not very helpful in grasping the true meaning of conversion. Peter is often described as headstrong. He demonstrated his bravado when he pledged unwavering loyalty to Jesus, a loyalty that wavered when a simple serving girl asked if he knew Jesus. The Bible does not emphasize the weaknesses of other disciples, as it does of these two men. Why is that? Perhaps the sacred text is making two important points. First, that God chooses misinformed and unreliable human beings. Second, that it is precisely through such individuals that God accomplishes great feats.

In the gospel reading, Jesus announces that his church will be established on Peter. Why was Peter chosen? There were three men who appear to have been Jesus' closest companions: Peter, James, and John. They are the ones who witnessed Jesus' transfiguration. They are also the ones who were present during Jesus' agony in the garden. These men also stand out as leaders in the early church. Peter was the apostle to the Jewish community; James became the head of the church in Jerusalem; and John is associated with the Christian community in Ephesus. We really do not know why these three were set apart from the others. Nor are we certain why Peter was chosen from among them. What we do know is that the church moved forward because of these three men, and that all looked to Peter as their leader.

If these three men were so important, why is it that Paul, rather than James or John, is remembered? Perhaps the very composition of the Acts of the Apostles, clearly divided into two parts, provides the answer. The first twelve chapters concentrate on the birth and development of the church in Jerusalem and the surrounding territory. In these stories, Peter and the mission to the Jewish community are prominent. Beginning with chapter thirteen, we read of how the gospel was carried beyond Jerusalem into the broader Roman-Greco world. Here Paul is the leading actor, and the Gentile communities become the focus of his ministry. Thus, Peter and Paul represent the spread of the gospel to both the Jewish and the Gentile worlds.

The first and second readings recount episodes in the lives of Peter and Paul. In the first, Peter is in prison; in the second, Paul is. In both instances we see how God works for the good of the church, through the agency of very human men. Peter was freed and delivered back to the Christian community, but not because of anything he had done to facilitate his escape. He had not exerted unusual power over his jailers, nor were his words so eloquent that he convinced the guards to release him. In fact, it seems that he did not even know what was happening to him. Later, he would acknowledge this to the members of the community. Paul seems always to have been eager to admit his weaknesses. He too had been delivered by God—not from prison, however, but from the isolation of standing alone at trial. Strengthened by God, he was able to carry on.

Peter preached the gospel to his own people, and Paul preached it to those outside of that community. And now it is our turn. Ordinary people as we are, with the various limitations that hamper us at times, we are the ones who today are to preach the gospel. We may not do it in any spectacular way, as these two remarkable men did, but we have the same power of God at our disposal as well. We may not be involved in direct ministry, but we can preach with our lives. We can show by the way we embody gospel values that we are indeed disciples of Jesus, and we can do this for both those who belong to our community and those who do not.

Praying with Scripture

- What opportunities for preaching the gospel does your occupation provide you?

- What are the human weaknesses that might hinder this?

- Today pray to Saints Peter and Paul for the courage to trust in God regardless of the difficulties you might be facing.

TRANSFIGURATION OF THE LORD (FEAST)

Readings:
Dan 7:9–10, 13–14; Ps 97:1–2, 5–6, 9;
2 Pet 1:16–19; Mark 9:2–10

I COULDN'T BELIEVE MY EYES!

"I couldn't believe my eyes!" It is an expression that we often use when we are happily surprised. We may understand it; we just didn't expect it. It may be that we awake some morning and discover that overnight the Earth was lovingly covered with a blanket of virginal white snow. Or we stand on the brink of a hill and behold a vista of yellow daffodils in a valley below. Or we open a package and find the gift that we have secretly desired for longer than we can remember. Then the expression comes to our lips: "I couldn't believe my eyes!"

The expression must have been in the mind of the visionary whose report is found in the first reading. The scene is of a cosmic throne room in the heavens, the throne itself engulfed in flames. And this is only the setting. Then the clouds part, and "I saw one like a Son of man coming, on the clouds of heaven." So often we concentrate on the identity of this mysterious figure, but to no avail. He is not really a weak human being (the Aramaic means "weak man"), but he is like one. What is remarkable about this vision is the commission given this figure by the Ancient One. Dominion over the entire universe is bestowed upon him. Unlike other kingdoms that rise and eventually fall, his will be an everlasting kingdom. Though conferred on him in the heavens, his rule will be exercised on Earth.

The expression must also have been in the minds of Peter, James, and John when they beheld Jesus transfigured before their very eyes. This was a man whom they knew. They had lived with him for a while. Even though they had witnessed the marvels that he performed, this was an overwhelming experience beyond the ordinary. Besides, other preachers had attracted crowds; other healers had cured people of illness. But this was something different. It was a transformation of him. And look who is with him —Moses, the one through whom God saved the ancient Israelites, and Elijah, the prophet through whom the power of God was demonstrated on Mount Carmel. Together they represent the law and the prophets, respectively. The disciples were so overcome by the entire religious experience that they did not want it to end. Then, as if this was not enough, they heard a voice from heaven identifying Jesus with the same words used at the time of his baptism (Mark 1:11). Who was this man they thought they knew? He is transformed before them; religious heroes from the past return to converse with him; and God identifies him as "my beloved Son." What were they to make of it all?

When it was all over, Jesus was there with them again: the same Jesus they had come to know and love, the carpenter from Nazareth. But was he the same? Or was it that they no longer saw him in the same way? Had it really happened? Or had their eyes and ears deceived them? Jesus' next words confirmed the reality of the experience. It had indeed happened, and he charged them to tell no one until "the Son of Man had risen from the dead." Now what did that mean? Son of Man they knew. He was the mysterious figure of whom the prophet Daniel wrote. Was that who Jesus was? That could explain the brilliance they had seen shine forth from him. If that is who he is, then maybe he will assume dominion over all the world, as Daniel's vision had promised. But what does "rising from the dead" mean?

Years later the author of the second reading recalled this episode as he explained the majesty of Jesus. At this point he knew what "rising from the dead" meant. He also understood how all of the traditions fit together to fashion an image of Jesus. Jesus was certainly the true Son of Man to whom dominion of the entire world had been given; he was also the Son of God, so identified at his baptism and his transfiguration. The author may have understood Jesus in this way, but, most likely, he did not really grasp the depth of meaning of these titles.

On this day that marks the glory of Jesus' splendor, we also commemorate the horror of another brilliance, that of the first atomic bomb explosion over Hiroshima. Those who witnessed this display must also have declared: "I couldn't believe my eyes!"

However, the meaning of that expression is different in this situation. Used above, it denotes marvel at the glory of God; used here, it is a response to the horror of human destruction. In the first instance, the body of Jesus was transfigured; in the second, millions of human bodies were disintegrated or disfigured. Now that we are aware of the power that we hold in our hands, these two commemorations call us to make a very serious choice. What will exercise dominion over our world? Will it be human force and destruction? Or will it be the gospel message of the Lord Jesus?

Praying with Scripture

- To what extent does God-given human ingenuity govern your life?

- What is your concept of Jesus, and how open are you to have it changed?

- Pray for the victims of war, both dead and alive, and pray for the understanding and tolerance we need for genuine peace in the world.

ASSUMPTION (SOLEMNITY)
Readings:
Rev 11:19a; 12:1–6a, 10ab; Ps 45:10–12, 16;
1 Cor 15:20–27; Luke 1:39–56

THE FIRST CHRIST-BEARER

The feast of the Assumption of Mary celebrates the doctrine that claims she was taken body and soul into heaven. There are no biblical traditions associated with this teaching of the church as there are with the ascension of Jesus. The earliest references to Mary's assumption appear as late as the fifth century, but the actual origin of the feast is uncertain. The readings assigned for the day do not throw light on the assumption itself. Instead, they invite us to reflect on aspects of Mary's life here on Earth, specifically the pre-eminent fact that she brought the Son of God into the lives of others.

In the gospel story, we see a pregnant Mary traveling to the house of Zechariah, where the child in her womb is recognized by Elizabeth and her own yet unborn child. Mary is pregnant like so many other young women of her day. In her pregnancy, however, she is the original Christ-bearer. We should note that she performs this honor in a very ordinary, unassuming manner. As she fulfills the routine responsibilities of daily life and makes an unremarkable visit to a relative, she brings the savior of the world to the people around her.

If anything is remarkable about this scene, it is Mary's prayer. It is not the type of prayer one might expect from a simple village girl. Instead, it has strong parallels with the victory hymns of Miriam, sung after the Israelites' escape from the Egyptians (Exod 15:1–18), of Hannah, recited when she dedicated her son Samuel to God (1 Sam 2:1–10), and of Judith, proclaimed after she saved her people by beheading the Assyrian general Holofernes (Jdt 16:1–17). Why would a peasant girl associate the birth of her child with the major liberation traditions of her people, unless she knew that he was their ultimate savior? This was not presumption on her part, for she was informed of her child's true identity by the angel who told her of her forthcoming pregnancy. Mary knew her religious tradition. Like every devout Jew of the time, she was steeped in messianic expectation, and so the prayer was in no way out of place at this time.

The very first verse of the reading from the Book of Revelation sets the context within which the woman heavy with child should be understood: "The ark of [God's] covenant could be seen in the temple." This verse calls to mind an ancient Israelite religious object of devotion that symbolized the presence of God in the midst of the people. Here, the pregnant woman represents the ark, and the child in her womb is the Anointed One of God. This woman, who is "clothed with the sun, with the moon beneath her feet" is thought by some to be the church, which brings forth the Risen Christ. He is certainly the presence of God in the midst of the people of all times. However, today another traditional interpretation of this image is intended. The ark is Mary, who brought forth the historical Jesus. He was certainly the presence of God in the midst of the people of his time. Both the woman in this reading and Mary in the gospel are Christ-bearers.

In proclaiming the gospel of Christ to the Corinthian Christians, Paul declares that Christ is "the firstfruits of those who have fallen asleep." This expression speaks of the end time in two different ways. First, "fallen asleep" is a euphemism for death; second, "firstfruits" refers to harvest, which is a metaphor for death. The firstfruits of a crop were important for two reasons. It was believed that they contained the most forceful expression of the life of the plant. Furthermore, they stood as a promise of more yield to come. As the firstfruits of the dead, the Risen Christ is the most forceful expression of life after death, and his resurrection contains the promise of resurrection for all who are joined to him. If Christ is the firstfruits, today we might say that Mary is the "second fruit." Her body was sacred, because it bore the Messiah of God, Jesus the Lord, and so she was granted the fullness of his resurrection before the rest of us.

Used today, the responsorial psalm extols Mary's glories. This unpretentious Israelite girl is now the queen of heaven. As such she is seated in a place of honor at the right hand of her son. There is a long tradition in spiritual theology that from her place of honor and privilege, Mary intercedes for us. While we may have many needs for which we petition her assistance, today we should be asking for the grace to be, like her, Christ-bearers in our world. She prayed that the proud would be scattered and the mighty cast down from their thrones, that the lowly might be lifted up and the hungry be given good things. Her prayer could well be a blueprint for our own ministry, as we bring Christ into our world today.

Praying with Scripture

- Examine your life to discover how you are nurturing the life of Christ within you.

- Reflect on Mary's prayer. Which one of the works of mercy might you make room for in your life?

- Is there any way that you might be a support to a young woman whose pregnancy is troublesome?

EXALTATION OF THE HOLY CROSS (FEAST)
Readings:
Num 21:4b–9; Ps 78:1–2, 34–38;
Phil 2:6–11; John 3:13–17

LIFE OUT OF DEATH

Who would ever think of venerating an instrument of capital punishment such as an electric chair or a guillotine? It seems so gruesome. Yet that is precisely what we are doing today as we celebrate the feast of the Exaltation of the Holy Cross. We are venerating an ancient instrument of capital punishment. There may have been a time in the past when our spirituality led us to spend long hours contemplating the suffering of Jesus itself. Some people even went so far as to afflict themselves with physical wounds. In some circles such devotion is still practiced. However, excruciating pain is not the focus of this feast. Rather, today we reflect on the cross, which was indeed the instrument of Jesus' death, because it brought life out of death.

The readings for this feast are filled with paradoxes. In the passage from Numbers, the people who have just been rescued from certain death in Egypt complain against God and Moses, accusing them of bringing them into the desert to certain death. Their carping forced the saving God to act as an avenging God. As a punishment for their insolence, God sent serpents, the bites of which killed many in the group. The people soon realized that they had brought this affliction on themselves by complaining, and so they repented. Following this, God directed Moses to fashion a bronze serpent and to mount it on a pole, promising that those bitten by the deadly serpents who looked upon the bronze serpent would be saved. And so it happened. The agent of death became the agent of life.

Almost every sentence in Jesus' instruction to Nicodemus contains a paradox. When explaining his own exclusive access to God, Jesus declares: "No one has gone up to heaven except the one who has come down." He then appeals to the wilderness tradition of the uplifted serpent to speak of his own being lifted up. As the serpent was mounted on a pole, so he would be crucified on a cross. The serpent symbolized life out of death, but he would actually bring life out of death. And the life that he would bring would be eternal life. Jesus must go down into death in order to come up into life, for life comes forth from death. It is no wonder that Nicodemus did not understand.

What follows is perhaps the ultimate paradox: God's love for the world is so great that God's only Son was sent into it to save it. By itself, this idea stands as an example of divine magnanimity. However, the literary context within which it is found makes it even more noteworthy. The reference to the bronze serpent recalls the sinfulness of the people, the agonizing pain suffered because of it, and the rescue from ultimate death that it brought. By employing this image here, Jesus maintains that sinfulness, suffering, and death characterize the world into which the Son of God has come. This traditional image and the characterization that it implies explain why God's Son comes into the world, but it also points to the way through which he will save that world. It will be through suffering and death. It was this death that gained us eternal life.

When Jesus declares that the Son of Man must be lifted up, he is, of course, referring to his crucifixion, which demonstrates God's graciousness toward us. However, the paradox is found in the meaning of the Greek word *lifted up*. It means "to be exalted." In other words, Jesus' being lifted up on the cross in pain and humiliation was really his exaltation. How could Nicodemus possibly understand this? How can anyone? It is a paradox, a statement that is seemingly contradictory, even absurd, yet expressing a profound truth.

The paradoxes in the passage from Paul's Letter to the Philippians enhance the description of Jesus' death. Though in the form of God, he took the form of a slave; because he humbled himself, God exalted him. The essence of the mysteries of the incarnation and the redemption can be summarized in just a few words, and yet the depth of their meaning will always be out of our reach. Nor can we comprehend the significance or the scope of Jesus' exaltation: "every knee should bend, / of those in heaven and on earth and under the earth." All of this mystery, all of this paradox is accomplished through the agency of an instrument of capital punishment.

With what sentiments should we celebrate this feast? How are we today to exalt the cross? On Good Friday we venerate a relic of the holy cross; many people kiss this relic as an act of devotion. But what of today? Two responses come immediately to mind: praise and gratitude: praise, because this is a day of exaltation—the wood of the cross is a sign of God's power to bring life out of death; thanksgiving, because we are the beneficiaries of God's boundless love.

Praying with Scripture

- Spend some time today reflecting on the message of God's love contained in today's readings.

- Remember how the self-emptying love of another person has changed your life, and pray that the same kind of love might grow within you.

- In what ways does your life "confess that Jesus Christ is the Lord"?

ALL SAINTS (SOLEMNITY)
Readings:
Rev. 7:2–4, 9–14; Ps 24:1–6;
1 John 3:1–3; Matt 5:1–12a

RSVP!

There are some events that we would give anything to attend. Who would not want to go to a presidential inaugural ball, the world series or super bowl, or the installation of a pope? Though very different, these are all momentous occasions and invitations to them are hard to come by. Tickets to such events are usually very expensive, more than the average person can afford. In addition to cost, one usually has to have connections in order to get an invitation to such an event. In other words, one has to be "in the loop."

Today we celebrate the most momentous event to which we will be invited, the great gathering of the saints in heaven. This event is more prestigious than a presidential ball, more exciting than any world series or super bowl, more momentous than the installation of a pope. The invitation to its celebration has been extended to all women and men "from every nation, race, people, and tongue." What kind of ticket does one need in order to get in? One must be marked with the seal of the servants of God. And what is that seal? The blood of the Lamb.

The vision described in the first reading provides a glimpse of this great gathering; 144,000 is clearly a symbolic number. It is twelve squared multiplied by a thousand. Twelve is the number of the original tribes of Israel. Since the Christian community appropriated to itself the identity of the people of God, the reference here is probably to that community. Both the squaring of twelve and the multiplication by a thousand are ways of indicating completeness; 144,000 suggests that the number of those saved is impossible to count. The gathering takes place at the throne of God in the presence of the Lamb that was slain and is now glorified. The celebration itself is one of praise of God, much grander than any ball, more electrifying by victory than any game, and more majestic than any installation.

In ancient Near Eastern mythology, the highest mountain was thought to be the dwelling place of the major god. It was from this mountain that the most-high god ruled over heaven and Earth and all that was within them. Israel appropriated this concept, claiming that its own God was the most-high god who did indeed dwell on the highest mountain. Over time, the hill on which the Temple in Jerusalem was built came to be known as that sacred mountain. Today's responsorial psalm asks who might be eligible to climb that mountain and enter the presence of God. Israel had a long tradition that identified those who could and who could not approach God. Known as the Holiness Code, it dealt with matters of ritual purity. At the heart of this tradition were issues of physical integrity and proximity to blood. One might expect that the answer to the psalmist's question would be taken from that tradition.

The actual response has nothing to do with ritual purity. Instead, the one who has access to God is "One whose hands are sinless, whose heart is clean, / who desires not what is vain." Sinless hands may refer to external conformity, but the image of a clean heart suggests a righteous interior disposition. In other words, access to God is not circumscribed by the Holiness Code; it is not limited to celebrities or those who might have connections. Everyone can be "in the loop," as long as that person possesses the right disposition.

The Beatitudes found in the gospel account remind us that the disposition needed for access to God is not equated with obedience to laws, regardless of how genuine those laws might be. Rather, it is brought to birth in our relationships with others. Jesus' teaching warns us about the abuse of power so often associated with the extent of our material possessions; it calls us to be meek and merciful; it challenges us to hunger and thirst for righteousness and to work for peace. Those who live in this way have access to God; they "can ascend the mountain of the LORD." They make up the multitude that stands "before the throne and before the Lamb." They are the saints of God.

We all know people who are living examples of this kind of holiness. They are the ones who stand tall in times of crisis, who step forward in times of need. They are women and men of principle, members of our families, neighbors among whom we live. They are generous with their time, their talents, and their material resources. They are patient and kind; they are forgiving and understanding. There is seldom fanfare when they practice virtue, but their virtue leaves its mark on the lives of those whom they touch. These are the saints we celebrate today, not merely those whose holiness has been officially recognized and praised. This is the multitude among whom we want to be numbered. This is the celebration to which we have been invited. Will we accept the invitation?

Praying with Scripture

- How do you prepare yourself for entrance into the presence of God?

- Who are the saints in your life? What makes them holy?

- Which Beatitude holds special appeal for you? Why?

ALL SOULS (COMMEMORATION)
Readings:
Wis 3:1–9; Ps 23:1–6; Rom 5:5–11; John 11:17–27

"IN THE HAND OF GOD"

There was a time when the "poor souls in purgatory" were more prominent in our theology than they are today. This does not mean that we have ceased to think about or be concerned about our friends and loved ones who have died. It means that we think about them in different ways. Our perception of the souls in purgatory is comprised of several different yet related theological concerns. Chief among them are an acknowledgment of human moral weakness, the concept of purgatory itself, and the relationship between the living and the dead.

There is no doubt that human beings are sinful creatures. Not only do we inadvertently make mistakes, but we are also guilty of deliberate transgression. Rather than think that people are either saints or sinners, it is probably more accurate to admit that there is good and bad in all of us, and each person struggles throughout life to hold these dispositions in the desired balance. Fortunately or unfortunately, there is no universally agreed upon determination of what that balance might be. Add to this acknowledgment of moral weakness the religious conviction that only the truly righteous should stand in the presence of the all-holy God, and the need to reform before death becomes obvious. But what happens if this reform is not completed by the time the person dies? Is the door closed forever to God's presence? Or might there be a way to eliminate one's imperfections after death? Trust in the ultimate mercy of God prompted Christians to believe that there was indeed a "place" where purification could occur. That place is purgatory.

Official belief in purgatory can be traced back to the eleventh century. Though this point of the tradition answers some questions, it raises others. If purgatory is a place, where is it? Perhaps we should think of purgatory in a way analogous to the way we think of heaven or hell. That is, it is less a place than a condition. Is the purification that takes place a process? And if so, how long does it take? This question implies that purgatory somehow exists within the confines of time. As valid as such a question might be, it arose during a period of history when we had a very different concept of space and time. Most likely new insights into science have played their part in our changing understanding of such purification. Many people today hold that life itself purifies us, and the final touches of such purification are completed in the act of dying.

There is a passage in 2 Maccabees stating that the living can make expiation for the dead: "Thus he made atonement for the dead that they might be freed from this sin" (12:46). This practice is also deeply rooted in Catholic tradition. If not even death can separate believers from the love of God in Christ Jesus (Rom 8:38), and if the living are similarly bound to that love, then death does not separate the living members of Christ from those who have died. Thus, there is a bond joining the living on Earth, the souls in purgatory, and those who are already in heaven. These groups have been referred to as the Church Militant (those who are still involved in the struggle), the Church Suffering (those undergoing purification), and the Church Triumphant (those who are enjoining their reward). This ecclesial bond prompts us to pray to the holy saints and for the suffering souls.

How do today's readings fit into this picture? The passage from the Book of Wisdom is often chosen to be proclaimed at a funeral. It challenges the long-held notion that death is always a punishment for sin, and the death of those who appear to be righteous is evidence that they were not. It also assures the living that the righteous dead are at peace with God, despite the fact that they may have been "chastised a little." Though this passage is not a statement about human immortality, it does say that the hope of the deceased is "full of immortality." The reading from Paul's Letter to the Romans also speaks of hope. Though by this time the people have a clearer understanding of immortality, the hope of which Paul speaks is not grounded in any enduring dimension of human existence but in God's love for us. Finally, the reading from John's Gospel brings together the love of God and the hope that death is not the end: "Jesus told her, 'I am the resurrection and the life; [s]he who believes in me, even if [s]he dies, will live.'"

The commemoration of All Souls is rich with meaning for all of us. It reminds us that as sinners we must reform our lives; it assures us that death separates us neither from God nor from each other; and it invites us to trust in God's unfailing love for us. Does it answer our questions about death? No! About purgatory? No! Then what does it do? It assures us that both in life and in death we are in the hand of a merciful, loving God.

Praying with Scripture

- Remember your loved ones who have gone before you in death. Commend them to the loving embrace of God.

- Spend some time reflecting on your own inevitable death. Trust that God will continue to care for you.

- Take steps today to reform your life and purge yourself of your moral weaknesses, to the extent that you can.

DEDICATION OF THE LATERAN BASILICA (FEAST)
Readings:
Ezek 47:1–2, 8–9, 12; Ps 46:2–3, 5–6, 8–9;
1 Cor 3:9c–11, 16–17; John 2:13–22

THE TEMPLE OF GOD

One of the most disputed religious spots in the world in recent times is located in the city of Jerusalem. Known as the Dome of the Rock, it is referred to by Jews as the Temple Mount, because it is believed to be the site where the ancient Temple stood. On the other hand, the Muslims call it the Noble Sanctuary, because it is believed that the mosque presently standing there houses the rock from which Muhammad began his journey to heaven. Despite the different religious meanings accorded this site by the two communities, they both maintain that this elevation is the same Mount Moriah on which Abraham built an altar on which to sacrifice his son Isaac. No religious shrine holds the same meaning for Christians as this site does for Jews and Muslims, not even St. Peter's Basilica in Rome. If any church in the world is considered the "Mother" church, it is the Basilica of St. John Lateran, the official seat of the pope. It is the commemoration of the dedication of this church that we celebrate today. This may seem like a strange feast. However, we are not celebrating a building, but the religious meaning of a religious shrine.

The reading from the prophet Ezekiel describes the temple as the source of life. It faces the east for the people believed that enlightenment, symbolized by the rising sun, originated there. Like the river in the garden in Eden (Gen 2:10), a river flows out from the very heart of the Temple. Its banks are lush with fertile fruit trees of every kind. This stream of living water is both the home of some animals and the nourishment of others. The life-giving power of God flows out from the Temple in a series of concentric circles. First is the stream of water from the sanctuary itself; then, whatever plant that water touches both receives the power of life and hands it on to the fruit that it produces; finally, the rich fruit is food to other creatures and its leaves are used for medicine. Thus the life-giving power of God radiates throughout all of creation. This same image is found in the responsorial psalm.

There is no question about the importance of the Temple in Jerusalem at the time of Jesus. Every observant Jew was required to journey there in pilgrimage to celebrate the Passover. This obligation sets the stage for Jesus' words and actions as recounted in the gospel for today. Since Jews came from all over the world to celebrate this feast in Jerusalem, there was a great need for exchanging Roman coins stamped with the head of Caesar for coins that could be used in the Temple. If this was an acceptable practice, we can't help but wonder why Jesus was so irate, lashing out at the merchants, accusing them of making the Temple a marketplace. But a part of the Temple was a marketplace. The transactions were legitimate. They were essential supports of the Temple service, and they were conducted in the appropriate Temple area. The story tells us that it was religious zeal that prompted Jesus to act in such a way.

The words that follow were heard by some as a blasphemous insult hurled at the Temple and, consequently, the God of the Temple. In justification for acting as he did, Jesus proclaims: "Destroy this Temple and in three days I will raise it up." This is more than a threat; it is a declaration of superiority. His suggestion that the Temple might be destroyed calls to mind the jeopardy in which Jeremiah placed himself when he simply foretold the ruin of the earlier Temple (Jer 26:11). Jesus then claims that after three days he will be able to rebuild the Temple, but, as the story tells us, he was talking about his body. The gospel writer makes this clear in the original Greek text where Jesus employs two different words for *temple*. One means *temple* generally, and this is the one that Jesus uses when he is speaking of the building. The other is used when referring to the inner sanctum of the sanctuary. This is the one Jesus uses for his body. Thus, he is not really talking about the building as such, but of the sacred section where the presence of God was believed to be, and he is identifying himself with that sacred presence.

In his Letter to the Corinthian Christians, Paul broadens the idea of temple even more. He tells his converts: "You are the temple of God, and…the Spirit of God dwells in you." He claims the right to say this because he himself was the master builder who, through his preaching, laid the foundation of their identity, and that foundation is none other than Jesus Christ himself. This temple image provides Paul with a religious basis for the development of his Christian ethic. If the Corinthians are temples of God, then everything must be done to assure their holiness. Since the Spirit of God dwells in them, they must be open to the promptings of that Spirit, and be transformed more and more into women and men who are worthy of their calling. This is the challenge placed before us on today's feast.

Praying with Scripture

- Does the church represent for you the source of living waters? If not, why not?

- Reverential silence is not always observed in our churches today. How has this affected your perception of the holiness of the church?

- What in your behavior diminishes your sense of being the temple of God?

IMMACULATE CONCEPTION (SOLEMNITY)
Readings:
Gen 3:9–15, 20; Ps 98:1–4;
Eph 1:3–6, 11–12; Luke 1:26–38

WHAT DOES IT MEAN?

"Hail, full of Grace! The Lord is with you." We are told that Mary was puzzled at such a greeting. Being a devout Jew, she was certainly familiar with God's mysterious presence in the Holy of Holies that made the Temple in Jerusalem so sacred. But this greeting was addressed to *her*. The Lord was with *her*. And she was a woman, not the high priest. Furthermore, she is called "full of grace" (the Greek phrase might be better translated *favored* or *graced one*). In what specific way was she favored or graced? There is good reason for her to be "greatly troubled at what was said."

If Mary was puzzled by the greeting, she must have been astonished by the message. She was told that the child she would bear would inherit the throne of his ancestor David. If that meant that he would be king, he would be a rival of Herod, the puppet king that already ruled the nation. With the recent history of royal family assassinations, the child's life would always be in jeopardy. Or did that mean that he would be the long awaited Messiah? But those who looked for a royal Messiah also expected some kind of political ruler. She was further told that she would conceive by the power of the Most High, and the child would be called the Son of God. Whatever did that mean? We do Mary a disservice if we think she truly understood this message. Her response shines forth as a beacon of brilliant faith and confidence: "May it be done to me according to your word."

Today is not the feast of the Annunciation, despite the fact that the story of the annunciation is the gospel reading assigned to it. We are not celebrating the conception of Jesus, but the conception of Mary. Furthermore, it is not simply her conception that we consider, but her Immaculate Conception. Actually, the feast has little to do with conception itself; but it has everything to do with Mary being "graced."

The need for grace is evident in the first reading. The man and woman have sinned and now they stand guilty before God. The punishments meted out to them are not merely temporary chastisements; they are permanent sentences that reach to the very core of their being. The woman who was fashioned from man suffers within her marital relationship with that man; the man who was formed from the ground suffers because of his tedious agricultural relationship with that ground. But there is also hope in that story. The offspring of the woman, a reference to the entire human race, does not succumb to the attack of the offspring of the serpent, a reference to evil forces. How this hope is fulfilled is not stated. In fact, it was not until centuries later, when the Christian community reflected on the extraordinary character of Mary, that her role in the fulfillment of this promise was sketched.

Hope and grace can be seen in the second reading as well. There Paul assures the Ephesians and us that this promise has indeed been fulfilled. We have all been blessed in Christ, made holy and without blemish. In other words, we are now "graced." Like the couple in the first reading, we have all sinned and we are all in need of the adoption by God. Mary, on the other hand, was "graced" from the very beginning. She was "graced" before sin could strike at her. She was "graced" because the one who is the true Emmanuel or "God with us" would be with her, within her, made of her.

What relevance might contemporary people derive from the theological meaning of this feast? The idea that God would preserve from any taint of sin the woman who would bear the all-holy Son of God was understandable to those who held that human nature was inherently corrupt. Very few people hold such a negative view today, and this does not mean that they deny that we all struggle with inclinations that lead us to sin. Nor do we today maintain that human sinfulness is handed down generation after generation through human conception, as some medieval Christians believed. Do these advances in understanding nullify the significance of today's theology? Not at all. It forces us to look beneath doctrinal statements and the readings assigned to this feast to discover their deeper religious meaning.

The feast celebrates an important moment in the story of salvation. The readings lead us through aspects of that saving drama. The passage from Genesis reminds us of our universal need for salvation; no one is exempt, because no one is free from sin. It also announces the promise of salvation. It tells us that there will be a woman, like other women, who will bear a son. But this son, who will be the ultimate representative of the entire human race, will vie with the forces of evil. We have a savior, and he came to us through a young woman from Galilee. This is the glorious mystery we celebrate today.

Praying with Scripture

- Consider all the times that you have been given another chance after having failed to be faithful.

- Pray for the grace to be as open to God's plan for you as Mary was to God's plan for her.

- In what ways might you be an agent of God's grace in the lives of others?